AUSTRALIAN SILVER

1800-1900

First published 1973 by

THE NATIONAL TRUST OF AUSTRALIA (N.S.W.)
123 Clarence Street, Sydney N.S.W. 2000
(Womens Committee)

National Library of Australia Card Number
ISBN 0-909 723-09-5

Typesetting and Negatives supplied by
Filmset Centre Pty Ltd, Brisbane
Designed and produced by
Production & Printing Services, Sydney
Printed by Macarthur Press Pty Ltd., Sydney

ACKNOWLEDGEMENTS

The publication of this book has only been possible with the help and assistance of the following people to whom we are greatly indebted.

Kevin Fahy, Esq., whose work and research on the Sydney silversmiths is well known, and who has spent many hours helping me read the proofs of manuscript and generally correcting my many mistakes.

Mrs M. Graham for the use of all her material and researches relating to the firm of Brush & MacDonnell, the Sydney University Mace, Flavelle Bros., and Messrs. Hollingdale's gold crozier for St. Mary's Cathedral and for reading of proofs.

Mrs F. Hodges whose late husband's work on the Melbourne silversmiths has provided the excellent biographies of the Melbourne makers.

Miss A. Bickford of the Museum of Applied Arts and Sciences, Harris Street, Ultimo; K. Hood, Esq., the National Gallery of Victoria; D. Richards, Esq., the National Gallery of South Australia and Miss R. Ransome-Wallis of the Goldsmiths Company, London, for the time and trouble they took to help me during my visits to their various collections. Tamworth City Council for agreeing to the loan of the Regan Collection of Australian Silver.

W. Wilkinson, Esq., of the Silver Lyon, Scotland.

K. Albrecht, Kozminsky Galleries, Melbourne.

N. Roberts, Esq., Moghul Antiques, Adelaide and his son, Peter for collating and arranging the collection and delivery of exhibits to Sydney.

For access to their archives and records and for the material used in the preparation of this catalogue, we wish to thank—

The Mitchell Library

The State Archives of New South Wales

The State Library of Tasmania

The Society of Australian Genealogists

Also, our thanks are due to all the private collectors, some of whom wish to remain anonymous, for the loan of their family treasures, heirlooms and articles from their private collections for the purposes of exhibition.

Our thanks are also due to Mr Rick Altmann of Malvern, Victoria, for the excellent photographs to be seen in this catalogue. Finally, my thanks to Mrs P. Currie and Miss S. Crothers for the typing of the manuscript, and to those members of the Womens Committee who made the publication of this book possible.

INTRODUCTION

Australia in the 19th century was made up of six separate colonies, New South Wales, Victoria, South Australia, Tasmania, Queensland and Western Australia, South Australia at this time included the Northern Territory. In terms of working silversmiths, only three colonies could support any number of craftsmen, namely New South Wales capital, Sydney, Victoria, capital Melbourne and South Australia capital, Adelaide.

The population of New South Wales by 1800 was approximately 5,000, by 1837, 76,793 and by 1851, 187,243. However, the census of 1857 gives the population of Sydney and its suburbs as 81,327, roughly the population of a small English town today. It was in this climate of a penal settlement up until 1851 with a small population of emigrant settlers striving to make a living, mostly from a scratch start, that a silversmith had to work. Pre 1850 silver by Sydney silversmiths must, therefore, in this context, be very rare.

With the discovery of gold in New South Wales at Bathurst in 1851 and the abolition of transportation, many new settlers flocked to New South Wales and the population rose to 751,468 by 1880, the year the railway to Melbourne was completed. By 1891 it had passed the million. Obviously the greater the population the greater the opportunities for working silversmiths.

In the case of Victoria, the first census taken in 1838 showed the population to be 3,511. In 1848 the population of Melbourne, now a city in its own right, had risen to 43,860 and by 1851 when Victoria was formed into a separate colony, breaking away from New South Wales, the population of the State had risen to 77,455. With the discovery of gold in Victoria the population of the State rapidly increased and in the ten years to 1861 it reached 540,322. By 1880, the year of the international exhibition in Melbourne, the population had risen to 862,346. In 1901 the population of the City of Melbourne had risen to 459,000 and that of the State was 1,200,000. It can be seen by the above figures that pre 1850 Melbourne silver is, in fact, very scarce, and I think in this context, it would be difficult to find a more important item than the Brentani snuff box (q.v.)

Although the colony of South Australia was founded in 1836, the population of Adelaide by 1860 had still not reached 100,000 and in the census of 1901, the population of the whole of South Australia was only 362,000. However, the discovery of silver at Broken Hill provided a good supply of raw materials for manufacturers such as Wendt and Steiner and probably accounts for their large output which cannot be assessed in terms of the population.

In terms of availability, therefore, any piece of pre 1850 Australian silver by comparison to colonial silver in general must be considered very rare. It is my opinion that few, if any silversmiths other than possibly Edwards, Steiner and Evan Jones, carried items of their own manufacture as stock in hand. Most articles executed in their workshops would be the results of special orders. The majority of pieces of Australian silver are, in fact, pieces commissioned for presentation rather than manufactured for general sale. Therefore, the total amount of Australian silver in existence is by circumstance limited.

Australian silver has a flavour all its own, the silversmiths being drawn from all over the world. In South Australia, for instance, nearly all the working silversmiths were Germanic by extraction but by incorporating their own national identity with indigenous animals and materials they found about them, they helped to create a unique form of colonial silver.

From contemporary advertisements it would appear that most working silversmiths with retail businesses carried imported silver or plated items as current stock, take for example the following advertisement by Mr J. A. Pace from the Adelaide Observer, 28th April, 1847, the style of which is common to nearly all pre 1850 silversmiths' advertisements:

From this it would appear that it was only the necessity of fulfilling immediate orders such as presentation trophies that forced the silversmith into producing articles locally, thereby not giving him the opportunity to order from England, the waiting time being approximately six months. This to a certain extent is a generalisation but I cannot think of one item, either described in current literature of the time or existent today, of pre 1850 Australian silver which is not a presentation piece in one form or another, other than, of course, Alexander Dick's flatware.

The flow of ideas, tradesmen and skills between these various capitals was slow, if non-existent, due to a communications barrier, there being no really viable roads or railways, the main method of transport being by sea. I have therefore divided the contents of this book into three sections based on three capital cities, with the addition of one major silversmith working in Tasmania, David Barclay.

The length of each maker's biography must not be taken as an indication of his standing in relation to other silversmiths in Australia. Facts are few and far between. As a result, some makers have very full and complete biographies and others, who may be equally fine craftsmen, have, I admit, only sketchy outlines of their silversmithing career. The illustrations have been chosen so as to represent a cross section of the maker's work and to provide an indication of the highest standard he was capable of achieving and it is on these that a maker's reputation must stand or fall.

Australia's two most prolific silversmiths are the South Australian silversmith, Henry Steiner, whose business in Adelaide had a considerable output of an inconsistent standard, and the Melbourne silversmith, William Edwards, a manufacturer in the true sense of the word, whose products are always good, various and interesting and survive in considerable numbers.

If I were placed in the position of having to define who, in my opinion, would be the best silversmiths in Australia on a State basis, my choice would be for South Australia—Firnhaber; for Victoria—Charles Bennett of whom very little is known, pre 1845 records virtually being non-existent, and William Edwards; and for New South Wales—Dick for his flatware, Brush and MacDonnell for monumental pieces and Qwist for sheer inventiveness.

I would like to make a plea to all antique dealers and collectors not to have the inscriptions on Australian silver removed. No form of date letter system was introduced into the hall-marking of Australian silver and makers such as Steiner altered their marks as their business progressed. It is only from dated inscriptions that we can identify these marks and so form a systematic progression of the marks used by a maker during his life.

In conclusion, I hope that this publication will stimulate interest in the subject and I see the next step as a progression to books on individual makers related entirely to separate states. I would be most interested to hear from anyone possessing items by Australian silversmiths, especially if they are not listed in this book. The prefix 'extremely fine', 'very fine', 'fine', 'good' and a general description indicate an order of quality based on my own opinion, the same system being used to designate rarity.

J. B. Hawkins,
J. B. Hawkins Antiques,
13 Amherst Street,
CAMMERAY. 2062.
AUSTRALIA.
October, 1973.

LIST OF BIOGRAPHERS

M.G.	Mrs Marjorie Graham
K.F.	K. Fahy, Esq.
J.B.H.	J. B. Hawkins, Esq.
F.N.H.	The Late F. N. Hodges, Esq.

CONTENTS

NEW SOUTH WALES SILVERSMITHS

WALTER HARLEY (Arrived Sydney 1815—Departed 1821)

HARLEY, Walter a silversmith by trade, was a native of Wexford, Ireland. Convicted at Dublin in 1813 for an unknown offence he was sentenced to seven years transportation. In October 1814 he sailed on the "Frances and Eliza" which did not reach Sydney until August 1815. During the voyage the ship was captured by an American privateer off the coast of Madeira and the ship's papers lost or destroyed. In 1817 he made application to Governor Macquarie for a ticket of leave claiming that for assisting the captain of the "Frances and Eliza" at the time of its possession by the Americans he had been promised a ticket of leave on arrival at Sydney. In 1818 he applied for a full pardon but it was not until January 1820 that he received a conditional pardon.

From the time of his arrival at Sydney until 1818 he was assigned to Mr Austin, a jeweller, and was later employed by the jeweller Jacob Josephson of Pitt Street. In October 1820 having left Josephson to commence business on his own account he advertised in The Sydney Gazette as a manufacturing silversmith at Castlereagh Street. In July 1821 he announced in the same newspaper his intention of leaving the colony by the earliest opportunity.   **K.F.**

1   An extremely rare pair of teaspoons with Glasgow marks for 1820, the town mark for Glasgow being substituted for a kangaroo. The crest of an elephant's head issuing from a coronet is that of Davey over his initials "A.T.D.", Lieutenant Governor of Van Diemen's Land 1813-1820. These are probably the earliest surviving items of Australian silver.

MAKER: W. Harley, Sydney. LENGTH: 15 cm
CIRCA: 1820 COLLECTION: P. Bell Antiques, Sydney.
ILLUSTRATED

Thomas Davey (1758-1823) was a native of Devon. In 1778 he secured a commission as a second lieutenant in the marines and served in America and the West Indies. In 1787 he was a volunteer guard accompanying Governor Phillip's First Fleet which arrived at Sydney Cove in January, 1788. His wife later claimed he was the first to land. He returned to England in 1792. After several years military service he secured the appointment of Lieutenant-governor of Van Diemen's Land succeeding David Collins who had died in 1810. He arrived at Sydney with his wife and daughter in October 1812 but did not take up his post at Hobart Town until February 1813. Frequently at loggerheads with his superior Governor Macquarie he was eventually replaced by William Sorell. He remained in the colony but despite considerable grants of land he had little success as a settler. In 1821 he sailed for England to present certain claims to the secretary of state and settle his private affairs. He died in London on 2nd May, 1823. His wife and daughter remained in Van Diemen's Land. *(Australian Dictionary of Biography)*

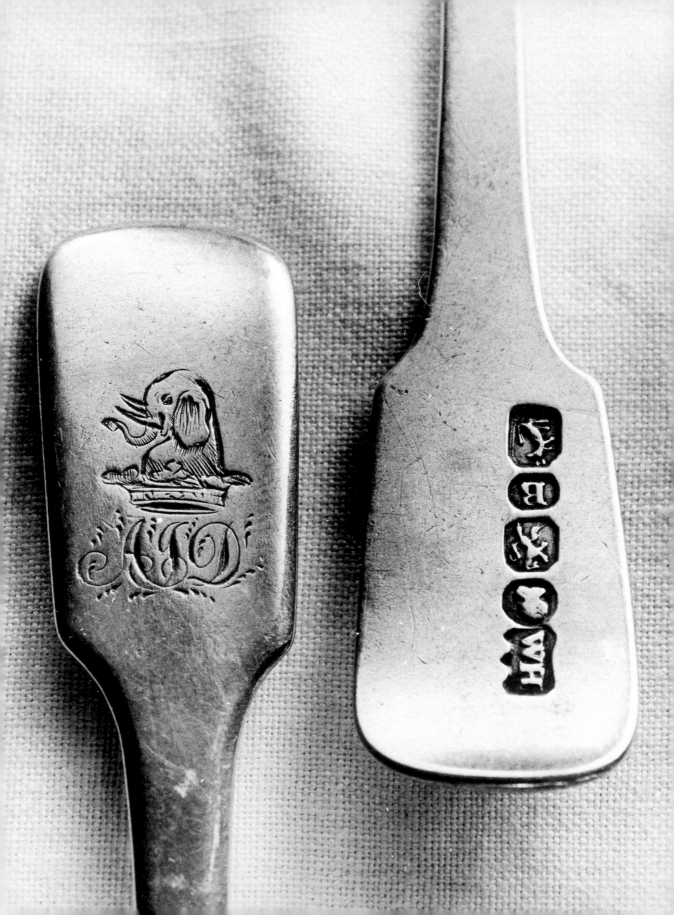

SAMUEL CLAYTON (Arrived 1816—Died 1853)

CLAYTON, Samuel was transported to Australia for 7 years, arriving in New South Wales on the "Surrey" in 1816. He advertises as a painter and engraver, "likenesses taken and instruction in ornamental painting and drawing given"; Sydney Gazette, 14th January, 1817. His business obviously grew, for in the Sydney Gazette, 15th August, 1818, he states, in addition to the above: "A variety of jewellery and silver work on hand, good prices given for old silver" at 80 Pitt Street. By 1820 he had moved to No. 23 Pitt Street. In the Sydney Gazette, 4th November, 1820: he advertises "Jewellery and silverwork made and repaired".

Clayton received his ticket of leave on 1st October, 1824 and married two weeks later by Special Licence Jane Lofthouse on 14th October, 1824. He had one son by his first marriage, Dr Benjamin Clayton, who practised at Windsor. Mrs Jane Clayton died in 1829.

Clayton was still in business in 1826. In The Sydney Gazette, 2nd January of that year he advertises at 23 Pitt Street. His will (Probate Office No. 2719 Series 1) made in 1831 leaves all his property in Great Britain, Ireland and New South Wales to his son and makes him sole executor. He advertises his business for sale also in 1831, but is still in Pitt Street in 1834, moving to Windsor in 1835. He died at Gunning, N.S.W., in 1853 leaving an estate of £1,000 as evidenced by his will.

The only recorded items by Clayton are the two trowels in the Mitchell Library.   **J.B.H.**

2   A good and extremely rare small presentation trowel inscribed "The gift of the Masonic Lodge, No. 260 Sydney N.S. Wales. To his Honour Lt. Governor Erskine Col. 48th Regt. C. B. Vice Patron of the Benevolent Society and President of the N.S. Wales Auxiliary Bible Society etc. etc. 1823." Engraved at the base where the handle joins the blade "S. Clayton Fecit" plus various Masonic symbols. To the rear "Mathew Bacon W.M. CCLX."

MAKER: Samuel Clayton. WEIGHT: 1½ ozs. LENGTH: 15 cm. WIDTH: 5½ cm.
CIRCA: 1823 COLLECTION: The Mitchell Library, Sydney.
ILLUSTRATED

A similarly engraved but larger trowel also by Clayton presented to Lachlan Macquarie, after his laying of the first stone of the Catholic chapel, 29th October, 1821, at present on exhibition at the Mitchell Library (Dixon Gallery) it is the only other recorded item by this maker from which the mark is taken for the marks' index.

ILLUSTRATED

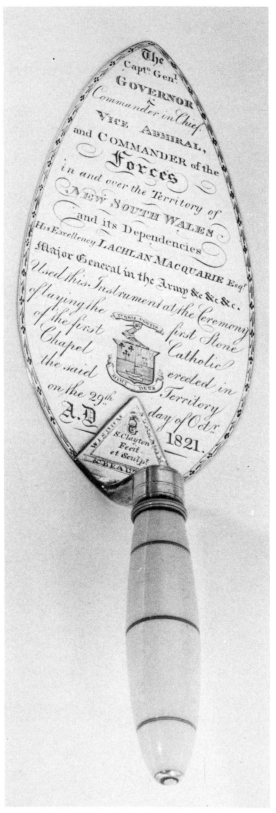

Item 2

JAMES ROBERTSON (1781-1868)

ROBERTSON, James born in 1781 in Renfrew, Renfrewshire, Scotland, married Anna Maria Ripley aged 32 at Stepney Church, London in 1808. He left England on the "Providence" arriving in Sydney, New South Wales on the 7th January, 1822 with his wife and six children, James 12, Catherine Maria 10, Brisbane 8 (this may indicate the length of Robertson's friendship with Brisbane), John 6 (later four times Premier of N.S.W.), Lavalette 4 and Sarah Jane 2. Two more children were later born in Australia.

Robertson came in the service of Sir Thomas Brisbane who succeeded Macquarie as Governor in 1822. Brisbane a keen astronomer brought his own private observatory to Australia, Robertson as keeper of clocks and instruments and Dunlop his private astronomer.

The Sydney Gazette, 18th January, 1822: "J. Robertson, Government Clockmaker, 57 Castlereagh Street. Notice—Mr. Robertson is appointed to the General Superintendence of Government Clocks throughout the territory with a salary of £30 payable from the Police Fund", only 11 days after arrival, this can only be attributed to friends in high places!

The Sydney Gazette, 6th February, 1823. "Maker silver tankard presented by Agricultural Society to Mr Bradley". (lost)

By 1825 has changed address to 6 George Street in Underwood's Building and in the Sydney Gazette, 28th September, 1827, we read: "The Paramatta Town Cup, valued at 55 gns. (lost) and the Junius Cup valued at 25 gns. have been got up by Mr Robertson of George Street with his usual taste and elegance."

Receiving a land grant in the Hunter Valley of 2,000 acres, Plashett Park, he seems to have retired circa 1830. however, he maintained his property of 86 acres in Sydney at Robertson's Point, being one of the first settlers on the North Shore. This property was sold to James Milson in 1853 for £4,000. He died at Aberglasslyn, N.S.W. in 1868.   **J.B.H.**

3   A rare and interesting set of six dessert spoons made for John Palmer who arrived Sydney as Purser on "H.M.S. Sirius" in 1788, later becoming Commissary General in New South Wales. He died in 1833.

MAKER: J. Robertson, Sydney. CIRCA: 1825
COLLECTION: Mr B. P. Palmer, N.S.W.

4   A fine and extremely rare racing trophy known as "The Junius Cup" inscribed: "The Junius Cup, Presented to Robt. Fitzgerald as the Winner by his Horse Creeper. John Raine, John Payne, John Fulton—Stewards." To the reverse: "N.S.W. Parramatta Racing Fund, October Meeting 1827. John Harris Esq., J.P., William Lawson Esq.,—Umpires."

MAKER: J. Robertson, Sydney. WEIGHT: Approx 15 oz. HEIGHT: 19 cm.
CIRCA: 1827 Private Collection, N.S.W.

It had a contemporary value of 25 guineas being presented by Mr W. Nash for a race to be run once around the Parramatta racecourse and was raced for on 3rd October, 1827.

Junius, the outstanding turf horse prior to 1828, was sired by Hector, the first pure bred Arabian horse imported into Australia. Formerly the property of the Duke of Wellington, he was imported by Robert Campbell of Campbell's Wharf in 1807[1]).

The race was named after Junius who was foaled in 1819. Mr Nash had tried to buy him as a foal but did not secure him until 1822. Under Nash's ownership, Junius proved outstanding. At the Sydney Turf Club Races on the Bellevue

Course at Bondi in 1825, Junius won the Town Plate on the first day and the Magistrates Plate on the second day. The first race, the Ladies Cup, was won by Mr Wentworth's Speedy. The trophy supplied by the local silversmith, Clayton, was of inferior quality and the committee gave Wentworth the choice of another local product or one to be ordered from London. Patriot Wentworth advised the Club that he "would prefer one made in this Colony although it may be inferior to one of English manufacture".[2] (lost)

The first Sydney Turf Club race meeting was held in 1826. The major race, the Brisbane Cup, a trophy donated by Sir Thomas Brisbane, (lost) was won by Mr Nash's Junius, who again won in 1827 and was second in 1828.[3]

It is interesting to conjecture whether Robertson was commissioned by Brisbane to make the Brisbane Cup. I have been unable to trace any record of this cup in Australia.

1. *"Spirit of Wharf House" by Charles Newman*
2. *"Turf Cavalcade" by Douglas M. Barrie*
3. *"The Sportsman's Racing Calendar, 1810-1842" the property of the A.J.C.*   **J.B.H.**

5   A fine and rare pair of Communion Chalices inscribed: "Presented to The Scots Church, Sydney by John Dunmore Lang D.D. Minister, 1826." The foundation stone was laid 1st July, 1824 and this building was demolished in 1929.

MAKER: J. Robertson, Sydney. WEIGHT: 14 oz each. HEIGHT: 18 cm. WIDTH: 12 cm. CIRCA: 1826 COLLECTION: The Scots Church, Sydney.
ILLUSTRATED

In the case of all the above itmes it should be noted that, although they bear the punch of J. Robertson as a maker's mark. Alexander Dick, who seems to have worked for Robertson from 1824-1826, would be in my opinion the actual maker. The punches of "N.S.W.", "Castle", "Anchor" and date-letter are identical to those on Dick's work stamped with his maker's punch, see Marks Index.

Item 5

MOSELY MOSS COHEN & CO. (1812-1895)

COHEN, P. J. aged 25, came free to Australia in 1828 on the "Alexander" along with Mr Spyer, 22 years of age, and they set up in partnership as Cohen and Spyer on 11th July, 1828, appointing Felix Lynn (q.v.) as manager of the jewellery department on 30th June, 1829. They went bankrupt in 1831. The only address from records being given as George Street.

There may be no relationship between Lewis Cohen, draper, of 1 Denmark Place, George Street; Henry Cohen, jeweller, 5 Denmark Place; and Mosely Moss Cohen & Co., 3 Denmark Place, this information being derived from the New South Wales Calendar for 1833, but they all have the same surname and adjoining shops.

However, the silver salver presented to Innes was sold by Mosely Moss Cohen in 1830 and bears a makers mark "H.C.", which I assume to be that of Henry Cohen. The Australian of 7th April, 1830: "Cohen, M.M., jeweller of George Street at Hymans the bootmaker, 3 Denmark Place, made a silver salver for presentation to Major Innes." Three years later we have M. M. Cohen & Co., does this mean that Henry and Lewis in adjoining shops have formed some form of loose partnership with M. M. Cohen or that P. J. Cohen, bankrupt in 1831 has joined M. M. Cohen to make M. M. Cohen & Co.?

From the Australian, 4th January, 1840, "a superb racing cup" is shown in his shop and in August he advertises that he has no connection with any other house in the colony. A tilt at John Joel Cohen (q.v.) April 24th sees an advertisement for the Silver Cup for the Mudgee Races (lost). He retires and sells his stock, Sydney Morning Herald, 22nd June, 1843: "Mosely Moss Cohen, jeweller, near Bridge Street will sell his stock on retirement from the retail trade."

From Mosely Moss' Death Certificate the following information may be gleaned. He died aged 83 on the 3/9/1895 at his house "Mossworth" in Cooper Street, Burwood, Sydney of influenza and exhaustion, occupation Gentleman. His parents were Simeon and Hannah Cohen. He was born in Birmingham in 1812, had spent 62 years in New South Wales, had married in Sydney at the age of 21 to Caroline Pendray and had five children, of whom three males predeceased him. In fact his date of arrival must have been between 1829 and 1830 as we know he was advertising by 1830 and yet did not appear in the 1828 census. The information on the Death Certificate was provided by his 40 year old son, Charles who, with the passage of time, had obviously got his facts muddled.   **J.B.H.**

6   A fine and very rare silver salver with applied cast border inscribed "To A. C. Innes Esq. J.P. as a token of esteem from the inhabitants of Parramatta, March, 1830."

MAKER: Henry Cohen. RETAILER: Mosely Moss Cohen, CIRCA: 1830
WEIGHT: 16 ozs. WIDTH: 28 cm. COLLECTION: The Royal Australian Historical Society.

ILLUSTRATED

The Cohen family have proved extremely difficult to dissect from early records, however, my researches have shown there are two distinct families, possibly three from 1829-1860 in business in Sydney.   **J.B.H.**

Item 6

JOEL JOHN COHEN (Arrived Sydney 1839—Died 1853)

COHEN, Joel John arrived Sydney on the 19th February, 1839 on the "Jessie" as a free settler with his wife and two children and opened a business in George Street. He later had five more children in Australia. He engaged Mr Salter the best watchmaker in New South Wales in 1840 and advertises a massive silver cup manufactured at the establishment and won by Mr Rouse at the Homebush Races 1842. (lost) The Sydney Morning Herald of 19th October, 1844: "J. J. Cohen, manufacturing gold and silversmith, watchmaker and optician, The Temple of Fashion, 479 George Street, has first rate London workman constantly employed on the premises". There seems to have been a lot of friction between M. M. Cohen and J. J. Cohen as both parties advertise against each other and that they are in no way connected.

The Sydney Morning Herald, 21st December, 1844: "Massive salver for Mr J. Simpson, the Police Magistrate, from the citizens of Melbourne, of which this was only a portion of the presentation". (lost)

J. J. Cohen died 11th June, 1853, leaving an estate of £9,000. Fords Sydney directory for 1851 gives J. J. Cohen & Sons and at least two of his sons, Baron Burnett Cohen and Francis Cohen worked for him. In Waugh & Cox's directory for 1855 the business is not mentioned so they must have split up and opened businesses of their own. B. B. Cohen died in 1883 and Francis in 1870. No item by the two sons has so far come to light.   **J.B.H.**

7   Circular salver with cast applied vine and grape border. Engraved centre with Australian animal motifs to crest and motto and inscribed: "To Sir Thomas Dowling, Knight, Chief Justice of New South Wales as a small but sincere tribute of regard from the Bar, Sydney, September, 1844." The engraving signed Wilson, Sc., marked on the back, J. J. Cohen, Maker, Sydney, N.S.W. (possibly Anglo-Indian hallmarks).

MAKER: J. J. Cohen, Sydney. WEIGHT: 48 ozs. DIAMETER: 13 ins.
CIRCA: 1844 Private Collection, Sydney.
ILLUSTRATED

8   A salver with cast applied border and feet by Emes and Barnard, London 1839 with applied and engraved plaque fitted to the back, engraved Cohen & Sons, Silversmiths, Watchmakers and Jewellers, Sydney, New South Wales. This salver may well have been fitted with a new base by J. J. Cohen as the English mark is in the cast border. It is engraved "Presented to J. P. Fawkner Esq., by the Officers of the Corporation of Melbourne as a token of their regard on the occasion of his retirement from the Town Council. March 19th, 1845."

RETAILER & ENGRAVERS: J. J. Cohen. WEIGHT: 18 ozs. WIDTH: 25 cm.
CIRCA: 1845 COLLECTION: The Mitchell Library, Sydney.

Item 7

ALEXANDER DICK (Arrived 1824—Died 1843)

DICK, Alexander was a native of Edinburgh, Scotland. The date of his birth is unknown but the evidence would suggest he was born about 1800. By trade he was a silversmith. His trade card decorated with the Royal Coat of Arms, indicating vice-regal patronage, signified that he was a watchmaker, jeweller, metal gilder, silverplate manufacturer and engraver. In the register of Scots Church and St. Andrew's Church his occupation is noted as either silversmith, goldsmith or jeweller. He arrived at Sydney on the "Portland" in October 1824 as a free settler and probably first took employment with one of the several silversmiths then active in Sydney. By 1825 he was conducting his own business although it was not until April 1826 that he advertised in The Sydney Gazette as a "Gold and Silver Plate manufacturer, Brass Founder and Plater" at Pitt Street.

On 2nd June, 1826 his marriage to Charlotte Hutchinson was celebrated at Scots Church by the Reverend John Dunmore Lang. This marriage was a link with one of the most important emancipist families in the colony. Charlotte Hutchinson was the daughter of William Hutchinson, a former convict, who became prominent in several commercial undertakings and was a considerable landowner and pastoralist who took an active part in various civic affairs.

Dick prospered and by 1828 was employing several assigned convicts including Alexander Robertson (q.v.) In 1827 "The Australian" noted that "a silver cup, which is to be run for at the next Hobart Town races, is being prepared by Mr Dick". (lost)

In May 1829 he was indicted with Thomas Jasper for receiving twelve dessert spoons on Christmas Day 1826 stolen by persons unknown from the residence of the Colonial Secretary Alexander Macleay. The principal witness for the Crown was Alexander Robertson. After a lengthy trial both prisoners were found guilty. Dick was sentenced to seven years transportation to Norfolk Island.

Among the Colonial Secretary's papers are several letters from Dick and his wife asking for mitigation of his sentence and that he be returned from Norfolk Island and assigned to his wife but it was not until February 1833 that he received a free pardon.

During his absence the business was conducted by his wife. On his return he soon moved to premises at 6 William Place, George Street which he occupied until 1837 when he removed to new premises in de Mestre's Building, George Street.

In April 1834 he made the Sydney Subscription Cup, valued at fifty guineas, which weighed 84 ounces and stood fifteen inches high. It was regarded as "a splendid specimen of what can be accomplished in Australia". Another major piece from his workshop was the Prize Cup for the winner of the first-class sailing-boat match at the Regatta in 1840 which was described as of "infinite credit to the colony, shewing as it does that we are not devoid of talent even in the finest branches of the arts". The present whereabouts of these pieces are unknown.

In August 1841, a month before the death of two of his sons from scarlet fever, Dick announced his intention of retiring from business, apparently because of ill health. His condition deteriorated and after a long and painful illness he died at his George Street residence on 15th February, 1843 and was buried in the Presbyterian section of the Devonshire Street Cemetery. He was survived by his widow and six of their eight children. His estate included goods valued at almost £9,000.

After Dick's death his widow continued the business for a few years. In April 1844, styling herself a jeweller, she advertised the George Street premises for letting. In October 1845 she advertised a general sale of watches, clocks and jewellery and in April of the following year the auctioneer Samuel Lyons conducted an auction sale of the remaining stock.

In December 1846 she married Francis Ellard, a widower, who had conducted a music shop adjoining her premises in George Street. She died in July 1875 and was buried with her first husband and two of their sons at the Devonshire Street Cemetery.   **K.F.**

(See "Alexander Dick—Silversmith", Descent, Vol. 6, Part 2, 1973)

9   An almost complete canteen made for George Toxteth Allen, monogrammed GTA bearing the crest of Allen, Thaxted, Essex, Bart; and Fenchurch, Middlesex, a demi-lion azure holding a rudder. Comprising 2 large basting spoons, length—30 cm. 5 dinner spoons, 12 dessert forks and one dessert spoon crested Allen but initialled REA and 1 mustard spoon. Total 21 pieces.

MAKER: Alexander Dick, Sydney. CIRCA: 1828. COLLECTION: Various.

ILLUSTRATED

Item 9

10 Part canteen, fiddle pattern, comprising one large spoon, 2 small spoons and a pair of sugar tongs, marked en suite and initialled JMH.

MAKER: Alexander Dick, Sydney. CIRCA: 1835. COLLECTION: Various.

11 3 pairs of Sugar tongs, monogrammed.

MAKER: A. Dick, Sydney. AVERAGE WEIGHT: 1½ ozs. AVERAGE LENGTH: 16 cm. CIRCA: 1835 COLLECTION: Various.

12 An extremely rare set of four wine labels, "Madeira", "Port", "Rum" and "Brandy", complete with original chains. This is the only recorded set of pre 1850 Australian wine labels and provides an interesting reflection of the standard of living then enjoyed in the Colony. These would rank as almost the ultimate in rarity to a wine label collector.

MAKER: Alexander Dick, Sydney. WEIGHT: 2 ozs (total) LENGTH: 4½ cm. WIDTH: 2½ cm. CIRCA: 1835 COLLECTION: Goldsmiths' Hall, London.
ILLUSTRATED

13 Two good long meat skewers with ring handles and plain tapering stems, initialled.

MAKER: A. Dick, Sydney. LENGTH: 34 cm. CIRCA: 1835 COLLECTION: Various.

14 A fine and large pierced fish slice, fiddle and shell pattern.

MAKER: Alexander Dick. WEIGHT: 4½ ozs. LENGTH: 32 cm. WIDTH: 7 cm. CIRCA: 1835 COLLECTION: Silver Lyon Ltd., Scotland.

15 Soup ladle, the crest to the front a falcon with a baronet's rope twist scroll and the initials AW.

MAKER: Alexander Dick, Sydney. WEIGHT: 7 ozs. LENGTH: 31 cm. WIDTH: 10 cm. CIRCA: 1835 COLLECTION: National Gallery of Victoria.

16 A good and rare christening mug, inscribed MAC in a wreath, with engraved reeded bands to the body, good heavy gauge.

MAKER: A. Dick, Sydney. WEIGHT: 7 ozs. HEIGHT: 8 cm. WIDTH: 10 cm. CIRCA: 1835 Private Collection, Adelaide.

Item 12

Item 18

17 A fine, rare heavy gauge silver pap boat, initialled GC.

> *MAKER: A. Dick, Sydney. WEIGHT: 6 ozs. LENGTH: 14 cm. WIDTH: 7½ cm.*
> *CIRCA: 1835 Private Collection, Adelaide.*

18 A part canteen by Alexander Dick, fiddle and shell pattern, monogrammed FMG, possibly Frederick Garling, Solicitor, (1775-1848). The photograph shows three sizes of flatware from this canteen—the large basting spoon, dinner fork and soup spoon.

> *MAKER: Alexander Dick, Sydney. Total 11 pieces. FORKS: Length .1 cm.*
> *SPOONS: Length 22 cm. Large basting spoon: Weight: 5 ozs. Length: 30 cm.*
> *CIRCA: 1835 COLLECTION; Various.*
> *ILLUSTRATED*

19 A part canteen of flatware comprising soup ladle, two basting spoons and sauce ladle. The two basting spoons by William Eaton, London 1837, the soup ladle and sauce ladle by Dick, these may have been copied in Australia to match, initialled "J & L McD" for John McDonald (1791-1874) who arrived free on the "Guildford", January, 1812 and his wife Lydia, born Sydney 1794 died 1864. The balance of this canteen comprising six dessert forks, six dessert spoons, six dinner forks and six teaspoons have not been sighted prior to the preparation of the catalogue and will be by either Alexander Dick or William Eaton.

> *MAKER: A. Dick, Sydney. CIRCA: 1838 COLLECTION: McDonald Family,*
> *Queensland.*
> *ILLUSTRATED*

20 A very fine heavy pint mug of 18th Century form. Presented to J. H. Potts by the Bank of New South Wales in 1839.

> *MAKER: Alexander Dick, Sydney. WEIGHT: 14 ozs. HEIGHT: 14 cm.*
> *CIRCA: 1839 COLLECTION: M. Marteri, Esq., Sydney.*
> *ILLUSTRATED*

"Resolved that the sum of Fifty Pounds be given to Mr Potts for the purchase of a piece of plate to be presented to him on his retirement from the Bank in consideration of his long and faithful services." *Board Minute, Bank of New South Wales, 1-10-1839.*

Surviving from this presentation is a four piece tea and coffee service and a silver tray, all with identical inscriptions, presumably engraved by Dick, but English. Presented to the Bank of New South Wales by a member of the family in 1960. This tankard may have been added by Dick to the original presentation so as to bring the value up to the above sum.

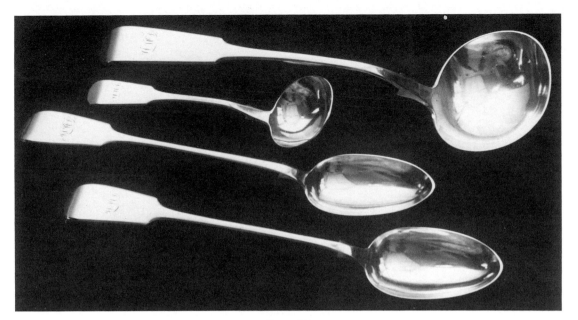

Item 19

Item 20

Joseph Hyde Potts: was born in Derbyshire in 1793 and arrived in Sydney on the "Elizabeth" on 5th October, 1816. He applied, and was appointed to the Bank of N.S.W. as "porter and servant", his remuneration being fixed at a weekly ration. He commenced duties one month before the Bank opened. He showed outstanding diligence, his educational background, mathematical grasp and well ordered mind, before long brought him increased responsibilities.

In 1819 he applied for permission to marry and bring his wife into the Bank building. The Board refused and it was agreed "in the event of his marrying to dispense with his services". Potts accepted the majority view. His artistic penmanship was being availed of by the Bank for the preparation of various official documents on which he worked in the evenings in the room on the premises.

In 1825 Potts position was "collecting clerk" and his salary £150 per annum. In 1826 the Bank commenced issuing new notes which were designed by Potts who was regarded as the finest penman in the country. Potts was identifying himself increasingly with the social and cultural life of the community. In 1825 he was appointed Accountant at a salary of £250. In 1830, for a sum of £505, he purchased 6½ acres of land situated on what thereafter became known as Potts Point.

In 1834 Potts married 19 year old Miss Emma Bates. A son was born and later a daughter but both died in 1838. This fact, and his own indifferent health, prompted him to retire the following year. On leaving the Bank, he took up residence at Surrey Hills and three more children were born. He lived also for many years at Homebush and lastly at Paddington. He died in September 1865, aged 72.

21 Gold snuff box inscribed "Presented to Captain J. B. Conbro by the cabin passengers of the ship Portland as a mark of respect and esteem for his urbanity and attention whilst under his conduct on their voyage to this port. Sydney, 1838". Inside the lid—"On this voyage the ship Portland conveyed to New South Wales, the Rev. Dr Lang accompanied by ten ministers, 16 Teachers and about 300 reputable emigrants, decidedly the most valuable importation that has ever arrived in the Colony."

WEIGHT: 4 ozs. 1 dwt and 10 grams. LENGTH: 7½ cm. WIDTH: 5 cm.
CIRCA: 1838 Private Collection, Sydney.

Lang married Alexander Dick. Dick is known to have been closely concerned with the affairs of the Scots Presbyterian Church. It would only seem natural, since we know that at this period, Dick was working in gold, that Lang would turn to him for the making of this presentation box. In my opinion, the gold standard is not sufficient for marking on the Sterling standard and this may explain why the box is unmarked. In addition, its new owner was returning to England on the "Portland" and Dick might have been worried as to adverse comment on marked gold boxes emanating from the colony in the English silver trade of a dubious gold standard.

22 A rare and fine foundation trowel. This trowel with simple silver handle of tapering rectangular shape and small blade, represents one of the few items marked by Dick and dated. Inscription: "Presented to his Excellency Sir George Gipps, Knight, Governor in Chief of New South Wales and its dependancies on his performance of the ceremony of laying the foundation stone of the Royal Exchange Sydney on Monday, 27th January, 1840, being the 52nd anniversary of the Colony".

MAKER: Alexander Dick, Sydney. LENGTH: 25 cm. WIDTH: 8 cm. WEIGHT: 6 ozs.
CIRCA: 1839 COLLECTION: J. Straiton, Esq.

ROBERT BROAD

BROAD, Robert probably arrived at Sydney in 1831. He is listed in Sydney directories between 1833 and 1839 as a watchmaker and jeweller at George Street. An engraved trade advertisement described him as a Chronometer, Watch and Clock Maker as well as a Real working Jeweller and Silversmith. He also carried on business as a draper. Apparently he encountered financial difficulties as in 1842 his estate was sequestered and in 1844 his city properties and household furniture were put up for sale by public auction.   **K.F.**

23   Teaspoon.

MAKER: Robert Broad, Sydney. CIRCA: 1835 Private Collection, Adelaide.

FELIX LYNN

LYNN, Felix arrived at Sydney from London on the "Swiftsure" 8th May, 1829. In June of that year, described as a working jeweller and silversmith, he was placed in charge of Messrs. Cohen & Spyer's jewellery department in George Street (q.v.). He is listed in Sydney directories for 1833 and 1834 as a jeweller and silversmith at George Street. In 1835 he sailed from Sydney on the "Leda" but returned on the "Midlothian" in July of the following year. He is again listed in Sydney directories for 1836 and 1837 as a jeweller and silversmith at Elizabeth Street.   **K.F.**

24   Dessert fork crested with "antlered deer".

MAKER: Felix Lynn. LENGTH: 21 cm. CIRCA: 1835 Private Collection, Sydney.

ALEXANDER ROBERTSON

ROBERTSON, Alexander a native of Edinburgh, Scotland, was born in 1790. A silversmith by trade he was convicted at Middlesex in December 1822 for forging silver hall marks. Sentenced to transportation for life he arrived at Sydney on the "Henry" in August 1823. In October of that year he was assigned to James Robertson (q.v.) but in May 1824 he was sent to the treadmill for an unknown offense. He was later assigned to the jeweller William Roberts for a short period. Between 1825 and 1829 he was assigned to Alexander Dick (q.v.). Following an altercation with his master he was sentenced to a flogging. Largely as a result of this incident he was the Crown witness at Dick's trial in 1829. In June 1831 he received a ticket of leave and was recorded in Sydney directories for 1833 and 1834 as a silversmith at Lower Pitt Stteet. He was later listed in Low's City of Sydney Directory for 1847 at 116 Castlereagh Stteet.   **K.F.**

25 A fine and rare mustard pot with applied gadrooned border to the silver gilt interior.

MAKER: Alexander Robertson. WEIGHT: 6 ozs. HEIGHT: 5 cm.
WIDTH: 11 cm. CIRCA: 1835 Private Collection, Sydney.
ILLUSTRATED

RICHARD LAMB

LAMB, Richard arrived at Sydney on the "Lady Fitzherbert" from London in September 1838. He commenced business as a jeweller in partnership with Clark Irving in November of that year. In December 1840 The Australian announced that "the business carried on as jewellers by Irving Lamb & Co. will be carried on after January 1st next under the style of Richard Lamb & Co." However it was not until January 1842 that the partnership of Lamb and Irving under the name of Richard Lamb & Co. was disolved by mutual consent. Plate and cutlery worth £42,000 was offered for sale. In 1844 Lamb was declared insolvent but he is recorded as carrying on business as a watchmaker and jeweller in George Street into the late 1850's. In December 1858 he announced his intention to retire, his address at the time being 394 George Street. Although he advertised importing English plate into the colony the evidence suggests he also manufactured silver goods locally. A contemporary newspaper reference described him as "that celebrated silversmith . . . of Sydney". Recorded items by this maker include a silver cup manufactured for the Goulburn races in 1848—whereabouts unknown.   **K.F.**

26 A fine rare and heavy covered silver entree dish in the early Regency style, with gadrooned edges and a chased handle. On the side of the dish is the inscription—"Presented to John Hubert Plunkett Esq. M.C. Attorney General By the People of New South Wales as a token of respect for his Public Character and esteem for his Private Worth Sydney March A,D, 1841", together with the Plunkett coat of arms and crest with the motto "Festina Lente" on the cover.

WEIGHT: 60 ozs. LENGTH: 28.5 cm. WIDTH: 21 cm.
COLLECTION: Museum of Applied Arts and Sciences, Sydney.
ILLUSTRATED

John Hubert Plunkett (1802-1869) was a native of Ireland. He arrived at Sydney in 1832 to take up the post of Solicitor General of New South Wales. In 1836 he was appointed Attorney General. Between 1841 and 1843 he was granted leave of absence to attend to family affairs in Ireland. He returned to his post which he held until 1856 and again in Sir Charles Cowper's ministry of 1865. He also served in the Legislative Council and the Legislative Assembly and made an important contribution to Australia's early legal and political history.

(See The Australasian Antique Collector, No. 14, 1973)

Item 25

Item 26

CHRISTIAN LUDWIG QWIST (1818-1877)

QWIST, Christian first recorded address from Sands Directory, 15 Hunter Street, 1864 he states that he is a gold and silversmith, he remained there until 1866. From 1867 to 1869 he gives his occupation as working jeweller at 11 Hunter Street. 1870 to 1875 as working jewellers (who was employed is not known), with a private address at Sharps Bay on the North Shore, but still at 11 Hunter Street. 1875 Qwist and Clarke, 171 Crown Street; 1876 Qwist and Clarke, 468 Bourke Street and 1877 Qwist and Clarke, 17 Hunter Street. His Death Certificate states, Christian Ludwig Qwist, died 21/10/1877, jeweller, of East St. Leonards, buried at the Necropolis Church of England cemetery, aged 59, born in Denmark, and had spent 25 years in New South Wales (therefore arrived in 1852), cause of death—pleurisy. He married Anne Price in 1859 and had five children, one boy predeceasing him. A little known but fine silversmith. Work by him is always good but very little seems to have survived.   **J.B.H.**

27   A fine large standing emu cup surmounted with blackened silver finial of an aboriginal carrying a spear with a palm leaf in his right hand standing on rocky clump with dead emu at his feet. The bowl with acanthus leaves, grape vine and hanging bunches of grapes and grape leaf handles and decoration, the base decorated in relief. This piece is unsigned but on the evidence of the following item, may be attributed to Qwist, both articles deriving from the same source and having identical base decoration except that one is cut intaglio and one in cameo.

   WEIGHT: 33 ozs. HEIGHT: 41.4 cm. WIDTH: 15 cm.
   CIRCA: 1865 COLLECTION: National Gallery of Victoria.

28   A very fine and rare ostrich egg claret jug of good proportion and design, the lid surmounted by an ostrich finial, the handle decorated with bunches of grapes, the vines and tendrils issuing from a Horn of Plenty, the whole of a good standard of workmanship.

   MAKER: C. Qwist. WEIGHT: 36 ozs. OVERALL HEIGHT: 47.8 cm. WIDTH: 14 cm.
   CIRCA: 1865 COLLECTION: National Gallery of Victoria.
   ILLUSTRATED

29   An extremely fine and rare claret jug and two goblets en suite made from mounted emu eggs silver gilt lined. The handle of the claret jug in the form of a twisted serpent chasing a butterfly (now missing) on the finial of the lid. Compare with the similar claret jug by E. & J. Barnard, dated 1860 of London. The goblets on simple stems with an entwined snake climbing up them.

   MAKER: C. Qwist, Sydney. DECANTER: Weight: 15 ozs. Height: 24 cm.
   GOBLETS: Weight: (each) 4 ozs. Height: 12 cm.
   CIRCA: 1865 Tamworth City Council, Regan Collection.

30 Unusual mounted emu egg in the form of a jewel casket on cabriole feet terminating in emu's claws, opening to reveal red velvet interior, surmounted by an emu in bullrushes.

MAKER: Attributed to Qwist, Sydney. OVERALL HEIGHT: 19 cm. WIDTH: 23 cm. CIRCA: 1865 COLLECTION: Ramornie Antiques, Sydney.

31 A very fine pair of large communion chalices of melon shaped design with silver gilt interiors.

MAKER: C. Qwist, Sydney. WEIGHT: 14 ozs. each. HEIGHT: 25 cm. CIRCA: 1868 COLLECTION: Congregational Church, Pitt Street, Sydney.
ILLUSTRATED

BRUSH & MACDONNELL (1850-1867)

BRUSH & MACDONNELL, 26 Collins Street East, Melbourne. (1858-1867)

W. MACDONNELL & CO. (1867-1891)

MACDONNELL & RODICK (1891-1893)

RODICK & CO. (1893-)

This firm, founded in Sydney in 1850 by Samuel Brush and William MacDonnell, followed the partnership Brush had had with John Flavelle—prior to the formation of Flavelle Bros. (q.v.) in that same year. Premises at 488 George Street were already in hand, and Brush and Mac-Donnell opened up in these.

The background of Samuel Brush is not satisfactorily explained; but he was primarily an optician, and the "working partner". William MacDonnell (born 1813), was a merchant already in business, and seems to have retained some interests outside the partnership. The firm set up as "opticians, watchmakers and jewellers", but added "Gold and Silversmiths" the same year. Silver and plated ware was imported, and early in 1851 Samuel Brush had returned to Sydney from a London buying trip. The accent was not yet on Sydney-made silver pieces.

Brush and MacDonnell must have gained the attention of the Governor, Sir Charles Fitz Roy, and their earliest piece may well have been the silver breast-plate made at the Governor's suggestion for presentation to Jackey Jackey (q.v.); the faithful Aboriginal who accompanied the ill-fated explorer Edward Kennedy.

In 1853 they advertised English-made watches of "pure Australian gold"; and before 1855 were supplying silver for various presentations in Sydney. One such piece was a salver, which was thought to be the largest of its kind in the colony. It is not always possible to say if these important pieces supplied by Brush and MacDonnell were made in their own workshop—some were English, with the engraved inscriptions added in Sydney. But the business had become established; orders for fine pieces were being received, and new premises were found at 179 George Street; approximately opposite the Bank of New South Wales' new building.

In 1858 the address was 326 George Street; Samuel Brush moved to Melbourne, and so in 1858 Brush and MacDonnell also appeared at 26 Collins Street, East. The partnership lasted until 1867—though the name was used in Melbourne for another year or so. (Brush was then in business on his own account; later continuing in Melbourne as the partner in "Brush and Drummond" (q.v.)). After 1867 the Sydney business was carried on as "W. MacDonnell and Co.", with the accent on jewellery and optical goods. (The firm "MacDonnell Bros.", though family connected, was not a jewellery concern—in fact the next generation of MacDonnells moved away completely from this trade.) Who the "Co." was, cannot be said; and though one Edward Lysnar (noted as a jeweller in Sydney in the 1850's), did work with W. MacDonnell and Co., following the formation of this firm, this was of short duration and Lynsar disappears again.

During the 1870's there was little change. William MacDonnell extended his other business interests, while in the 1880's the jewellery side of the business was gradually overtaken by the importing and retailing of scientific instruments. There were two addresses in 1880—the old 326, and also 312 George Street; the latter being the only address by 1882.

William MacDonnell died at his home at Balmain, in July, 1883, and by the end of the decade W. MacDonnell and Co. had moved to 262 George Street as "Opticians and Scientific Repository", In 1891 the name was "MacDonnell and Rodick". John Rodick had earlier been a watchmaker, and may have worked in this capacity for W. MacDonnell and Co. Whatever the position, by 1893 the business as it stood was solely that of John Rodick, and the name "Mac-Donnell" no longer appeared in any related trade.

Pieces made by Brush and MacDonnell include the following:—

1 Gold Trowel—Used at the Laying of the Foundation Stone of Sydney Royal Exchange Building. (1853.) *(Inscribed and perspective of building engraved on verso.—lost)*
2 Silver Salver—Presentation to J. H. Black; Retiring Cashier Bank of N.S.W. (1854). *(Inscribed and Embossed and Chased in Traditional Style.—lost)*   **M.G.**

32   An extremely fine and rare ceremonial mace.

MAKER: Brush & MacDonnell, Sydney. LENGTH: 102 cm. WIDTH: 23 cm.
CIRCA: 1854 COLLECTION: The University of Sydney.
ILLUSTRATED

The Archives of the University of Sydney contain correspondence relating to the acquisition of the ceremonial Mace; and the story commences with a letter written on 17th August, 1852, by Sir Charles Nicholson, Bart., in his capacity of Vice-Provost of the University. The letter was addressed to the Colonial Secretary of New South Wales, and the correspondence led to the Governor Sir Charles Fitz Roy being authorised to present the Mace on behalf of Her Majesty Queen Victoria.

There was a long tradition associated with the carrying of a mace upon university and parliamentary special occasions in England, and the mace which was made for the University of Sydney reflects the styling of those of earlier date in the possession of various English cities.

It is recorded on 4th September, 1854, that three guineas was paid to "Flavelle and Co." (q.v.) for a drawing of a design for the Mace: and we do know that it was in existence in the first week of December, 1854; when it was exhibited at the request of the Governor. There is also a contemporary statement that the design was that of the Colonial Architect, E. T. Blacket, Esq., who was already engaged as architect for the University buildings.

The Mace was made by Brush and MacDonnell, jewellers and silversmiths of George Street, Sydney: it weighed "upwards of 100 ounces", and was said to be the largest piece of silver-work yet made in the colony. The baton was of polished myall wood, with silver fittings, and the crown which formed the head, was of "solid silver". The cap beneath the crown proper, was of "frosted silver"—and this is the earliest reference so far known to frosting of Australian worked silver.

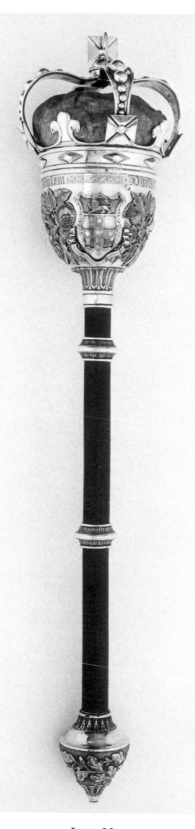

Item 32

The engravings of the Coats-of-Arms on the Mace are a history in themselves. When first made, the Mace carried the Royal Arms, and those of New South Wales as these were then accepted. But, it was explained, the final panel was allowed to remain blank, as the University had not yet received a Grant of Arms. The Senate adopted the design for the University Arms in December, 1856, and the formal Grant is dated 14th May, 1857. The engraving of the University Arms therefore, must surely have been done at some time after May, 1857; and the Mace is known to have been in regular ceremonial use by 1864—perhaps earlier.

(It is worth noting that this is believed to be the only occasion upon which the Mace has been publicly exhibited since it was first shown in 1854.) **M.G.**

33 A fine and rare silver breast plate presented by the Governor, Sir Charles Fitz Roy to the aboriginal, Jackey Jackey, inscribed "Presented by His Excellency Sir Charles Augustus Fitz Roy, Governor of New South Wales, to Jackey Jackey, an aboriginal native of that Colony. In testimony of the fidelity with which he followed the late Assistant Surveyor E. B. C. Kennedy, throughout his exploration of York Peninsula in the year 1848; the noble daring with which he supported that lamented Gentleman, when mortally wounded by the natives of Escape River, the courage with which, after having affectionately tended the last moments of his Master, he made his way through hostile tribes and an unknown country, to Cape York; and finally the unexampled sagacity with which he conducted the succour that there awaited the expedition to the rescue of the other survivors of it, who had been left at Shelbourne Bay."

MAKER: Brush & MacDonnell. WEIGHT: 5 ozs. WIDTH: 15 cm.
CIRCA: 1851 COLLECTION: The Mitchell Library, Sydney.
ILLUSTRATED

34 An extremely fine and rare centrepiece, known as the Cooper vase.

RETAILERS: Brush & MacDonnell. WEIGHT: 346 ozs. HEIGHT: 63 cm.
CIRCA: 1854 COLLECTION: The Museum of Applied Arts & Sciences, Sydney.

In April, 1854, the Sydney Press was unanimous in its praise for a "very large and elegant flower vase" on view at the establishment of Messrs. Brush and MacDonnell in George Street. The vase was of pure silver; weighed "upwards of 300 ounces", and stood over two feet in height. Much admired was the rustic design of fruiting vine; and even more so, the bouquet resting in the ruby glass liner. The "bouquet" was one of the celebrated feather ones, made by the nuns in Valparaiso. Sydneysiders were impressed.

The story of this magnificent piece begins in January, 1853, when following a most successful year's trading the six directors of the Bank of New South Wales were voted a testimonial. The vase displayed by Brush and MacDonnell bore an inscription to this effect, and was a presentation to Daniel Cooper, Esq.—one of the six directors.

It is known from existing correspondence that an order for such a vase was placed in London: but the vase we know to-day, carries no London Hall Mark, with maker and date; which normally would have been placed on a piece so important as this.

Also, the vase we know, carries a Coat-of-Arms on the plinth—not a presentation inscription—and the Arms are those of "Cooper" impaling "Hill". (Daniel Cooper married Elizabeth Hill of Sydney in September, 1846.)

The style in which the Arms are rendered—surrounded by the Collar of the Order of St. Michael and St. George, and no supporters—would indicate that the engraving was done not before 1880, and not later than 1887. The other possibility is that the Arms were engraved as early as 1863. when Sir Daniel Cooper, Knight, was created First Baronet of Woollahra: the Collar being added at the later date already suggested. However, this is perhaps not so likely an explanation.

(Sir) Daniel Cooper was born in County Lancaster in 1821: he was one of the Senate of Sydney University: a member of the New South Wales Legislative Assembly in 1849, and was elected its first Speaker in 1856. He died at Kensington, London, in June, 1902. **M.G.**

Item 32 (detail)

Item 33

EVAN JONES (1846-1917)

JONES, Evan was born in London about 1846 the son of Evan Jones, a tailor, and his wife Sophie Furby. He arrived at Sydney about 1855 and was later apprenticed to a goldsmith in Hunter Street. About 1868 he married Rose Lawrence. He is listed in a Sydney directory for 1873 as conducting his own business as a jeweller at 15 Hunter Street, premises that had been occupied between 1864 and 1866 by Christian L. Qwist (q.v.) another well known silversmith of the period.

Between 1875 and 1892 he is variously described as a goldsmith, jeweller or watchmaker at 11 Hunter Street. These premises had also been occupied by Qwist between 1867 and 1873. During the 1880's he established several branches in the city but by the 1890's his principal workshop was in Erskine Street.

He was active for many years in public affairs. In 1882 he became an alderman of the city of Sydney, a post he held for six years. In 1900 he was re-elected to the city council and continued as a member until his death at Mosman in May 1917. He was survived by his wife and their six children.

He was certainly the most prominent silversmith in Sydney during the second half of the nineteenth century and his work won many awards at exhibitions in Sydney, Melbourne, Adelaide and Brisbane. Apart from numerous racing trophies he produced medals, tea and coffee services, mounted emu eggs, jewellery, watches and many other items. An inkstand presented to Pope Pius IX and a salver of Australian gold presented to John Henry Newman on his elevation to the cardinalate were from his workshop as was the gold crown for King George of Tonga.   **K.F.**

35   A fine and interesting art nouveau style mounted silver emu egg.

MAKER: Evan Jones, Sydney. OVERALL WEIGHT: 8 ozs. HEIGHT: 26 cm. CIRCA: 1870 COLLECTION: Mr & Mrs J. D. Altmann, Melbourne.

36   A fine and large silver epergne inscribed—"Presented To W. K. Lochhead, Esq By the Officers and Members of the N.S.W. Seamen's Union in recognition of disinterested and invaluable services rendered in acting as Mediator and in so doing settling the dispute between the A.S.N.Co., and their Employees re the employment of Chinese Feb. 3rd 1879". It cost between £70 and £80 in 1878 and had been on display for at least 2 years.

HEIGHT: 106 cm. WEIGHT: approx 400 oz. CIRCA: 1877 Private Collection, Sydney ILLUSTRATED

(See The Australasian Antique Collector No. 14, 1973)

37   A fine, unusual table comport, the bowl a natural shell supported in stylised leaves, flowers and foliage on trunk stem and marked on the oval base.

MAKER: Evan Jones, Sydney. HEIGHT: 14 cm. MAXIMUM WIDTH: 30 cm. CIRCA: 1880 Private Collection, Adelaide.

Item 36

38 A fine and unusual silver mounted jewel box with inset silver scene of an emu and kangaroo raised on a palm trunk stem.

MAKER: Evan Jones, Sydney. WEIGHT: 15 ozs. HEIGHT: 24 cm. WIDTH: 19 cm. CIRCA: 1880 Private Collection, Victoria.

39 Embossed shooting trophy, the goblet mounted on three crossed muskets. Inscription removed.

MAKER: Evan Jones, Sydney. WEIGHT: 7 ozs. HEIGHT: 18 cm. CIRCA: 1880 COLLECTION: Mr & Mrs J. D. Altmann, Melbourne.

40 A good plain mug engraved with a picture of S. S. Northumbria and to the reverse "J.M. 1885".

MAKER: Evan Jones, Sydney. WEIGHT: 18 ozs. HEIGHT: 13 cm. CIRCA: 1885 Tamworth City Council, Regan Collection.

41 Extremely fine and rare four piece tea service, depicting a scene at the Sunny Corner Mine. Each piece bears the same inscription and the same embossed scene.
Inscription: "Presented to W. R. Hurley, Esq., by the residents of Sunny Corner as a token of their appreciation of his distinguished services as the pioneer of silver mining in New South Wales and the high esteem in which he is held as a citizen, 1886".

COFFEE POT: Wt.: 24 ozs. Hgt.: 25 cm. Wd.: 24 cm. TEAPOT: Wt.: 20 ozs. Hgt.: 21 cm. Wd.: 24cm. SUGAR BOWL: Wt.: 15 ozs. Hgt.: 18 cm. Wd.: 21cm. MILK JUG: Wt.: 7 ozs. Hgt.: 11 cm. Wd.: 16 cm. MAKER: Evan Jones, Sydney. CIRCA: 1885 COLLECTION: Mr & Mrs J. D. Altmann
ILLUSTRATED

42 Extremely fine bachelor teapot made from an emu egg with simulated wood handle and emus head spout, standing on three emu's clawed feet to a circular base. The whole surmounted by emu finial and with silver gilt interior. The whole concept of the mounting of this egg is unique in Australian silver and bears comparison with some of the finest continental work. Originally part of a three piece tea service—for the cream jug, see next entry—the sugar bowl is missing.

MAKER: Evan Jones, Sydney. OVERALL WEIGHT: 14 ozs. HEIGHT: 19 cm. CIRCA: 1870 COLLECTION: F. McDonald, Esq., Sydney.
ILLUSTRATED

43 A cream jug en suite with the above.

MAKER: Evan Jones, Sydney. OVERALL WEIGHT: 5 ozs. HEIGHT: 9 cm. CIRCA: 1870 Tamworth City Council, Regan Collection.

44 A tall presentation trophy with embossed shooting scene to the front.

MAKER: Evan Jones. WEIGHT: 20 ozs. HEIGHT: 31 cm. CIRCA: 1875 Private Collection, Sydney.

Item 42

FLAVELLE & BRUSH (1846-1850)

FLAVELLE BROS. (1850-1856)

FLAVELLE BROS. & CO. (1856-1869)

FLAVELLE BROS. & ROBERTS (1869-1888)

FLAVELLE & ROBERTS (1888-1899)

FLAVELLE BROS. LTD. 1900

This firm was founded in 1846, as "Flavelle and Brush", with premises at 87 King Street, Sydney: moving by the middle of 1848, to 488 George Street, "Opposite the Barrack Gate". The partners were opticians; so it was a short step from spectacle frames to jewellery making. (Actually in Sydney at the time, the two things were often combined.)

The partners were John Flavelle and Samuel Brush: but in 1850, on the formation of "Flavelle Bros.", Brush was left in possession of the premises at 488, which then became the first address of another partnership known as "Brush and MacDonnell" (q.v.), while Flavelle Bros. opened up their shop at No. 478.

John Flavelle (born 1816 or 1817), appears to have made his way to Sydney via Launceston— he certainly was a passenger on the brig "William", which arrived in Port Jackson on 17th May, 1844—and a Channel Islands family background could be suggested. He busied himself in Sydney, and a few months after arriving, consigned a case of tortoise-shell to Liverpool— perhaps for spectacle frames? His business partnerships in Sydney followed.

John Flavelle did visit London to select silverware and jewellery; but his life was spent in Sydney. His brother Henry (born 1814), was the "home partner", and though there is some evidence that Henry was briefly in Sydney, he was not a permanent resident.

By the end of 1850, Flavelle Bros, were requiring an apprentice; employing assistants, and offering to make any article of plate or jewellery to order. The Sydney market was fiercely competitive, and Flavelle's announced that the California gold wedding rings they sold were of better quality than the English—also their own stamp would be placed upon them.

Between 1853 and 1854 a more desirable position was obtained at 203 George Street. (Later re-numbered as "354".)

Also in the mid 'fifties Flavelle Bros., were selling mathematical instruments and photographic "apparatus"; it was no doubt this diversity which was the essence of their long survival in business.

About the end of 1856 the firm was known as "Flavelle Bros., and Co.", and though not immediately named, it can be accepted that the "Co." was John Roberts, a jeweller by trade, who lived close to John Flavelle in Lower Fort Street. (He remained there for many years after Flavelle had moved away from his city residence.)

In 1869 John Roberts was a full partner, with the firm's name now appearing as "Flavelle Bros., and Roberts". This styling was long-lasting: though in 1882 the address was 340 George Street. There was also a branch in Queen Street, Brisbane, and that in Ely Place, London, was in the care of Henry Flavelle. In January, 1888, Henry died in London; shortly after the firm had been re-named "Flavelle and Roberts", and a change of partnership was made by bringing in the younger Sydney Flavelles (Henry and William), while still retaining the firm's styling.

A new limited company was formed in 1892; in June, 1899, the original John Flavelle died at his home, "Wellbank", in Concord, Sydney; and by 1900 the name was "Flavelle Bros. Ltd.". During the Edwardian period a Vice-Regal Appointment was held; but following the end of the

First World War, the jewellery business concentrated in Sydney, was discontinued. Another partnership may be traced through Lismore and Sydney, while a new company was formed—still using the family name, but whose business was solely with dental supplies. (This trend had been commenced by the original jewellery firm in 1879-1880). In this way the name "Flavelle" still continues in Sydney; while the founding family is commemorated by Flavelle and Wellbank Streets in Concord.

There are contemporary references to Messrs. Flavelle designing presentation silver for manufacture in London, but fine pieces were designed and made in Sydney too. . .

A Tea Service—Emu Eggs—Silver mounted: chased, engraved & cast (1879.)—lost
Figures for Centre-pieces—Cast in silver from models. (1879.)—lost
Anniversary Regatta Centennial Cup—Presented as a Prize—(to a design by Barlow and Roskell, Sydney architects.) (1888.)—lost   **M.G.**

EDWARD JOSEPH HOLLINGDALE (1832-1882)

HOLLINGDALE, Edward Joseph. It is likely that he was the son of a young English couple who migrated to Sydney in 1832. In any case, Edward Hollingdale was born late in that year, and established himself in business as a watchmaker in 1854. At first he worked in Wooloomooloo and Pyrmont; and he was young when he married. He must have been a good workman, for in March, 1859, he was able to buy out Mr Asher Jude, a jeweller of 102 King Street, Sydney. Mr Jude's stock was auctioned the following month, and he departed for Melbourne to set up another business there. The premises "next to the Rainbow Tavern" were moved into by the young Mr Hollingdale, who remained on this site and prospered. The business was to embrace all branches of the jewellery trade; with local and imported wares; and later the name "Goldsmith's Hall" was adopted.

Edward Hollingdale was a generous supporter of his church, and among other things, was for twelve years a treasurer of the St. Mary's Cathedral Building Fund—after the disastrous fire of June, 1865. It seems fitting that perhaps the finest piece to come from the workshop of E. J. Hollingdale, was the crozier made in 1877 for presentation to the then Catholic Archbishop Coadjutor of Sydney, the Most Reverend Roger Vaughan. The crozier of colonial gold, and myall wood shaft, was much admired, and the Committee who had called tenders for the making was more than happy with the handsome result. The crozier was also the first of its kind to be made in the colonies.

In 1879-1880, the King Street premises were extended, and early in 1882 the firm had become "E. J. Hollingdale and Son". But Edward Hollingdale grieved the loss of his wife, and he suffered ill-health, and died at his daughter's home in October, 1882. He was aged fifty. His funeral moved from St. Mary's Cathedral; where he had been present the month before at the official opening ceremonies.

His only son, E. J. Hollingdale, Junior, continued the business in King Street, which in 1898 was "E. J. Hollingdale and Kessel." The initials were later dropped, the firm continuing as "Hollingdale and Kessel".   **M. G.**

45 A fine and extremely rare gold crozier of standard form. For details of production and history see previous biography.

MAKER: E. J. Hollingdale, Sydney. LENGTH: 179 cm. MAX. WIDTH: 17 cm. CIRCA: 1877 COLLECTION: St. Mary's Cathedral, Sydney.
ILLUSTRATED

Item 45

JOHN McLEAN (1860-1872)

J. McLEAN & SONS (1872-1874)

J. McLEAN & SON (1874-1896)

McLEAN, John was in business for himself in 1860 at 145 York Street, Sydney, and described himself as: "electro-plater and gilder". By 1863 he had moved to number 74, and was silversmithing; while steadily building up and improving the electro-plating part of his business.

Between 1867 and 1878 McLean was at 70 York Street, but in 1872 his two sons (Edward and John, Junr.) had been included in the firm as: "John McLean and Sons". In 1874 only Edward was in partnership, and the name changes to: "J. McLean and Son". (It also appears without the prefixing "J".)

In 1869 McLean had received a "Highly Commended" award for his electro-plated ware; and between 1870 and 1876 had been given five First Prizes for this at New South Wales exhibitions. The firm was proud of this line, and advertised their plating by "Steam Power", and the plated wares were no doubt the mainstay of their business.

The peak period seems to have been in the 1870's. Silversmithing was not neglected, and the advertisements refer to Volunteer Ornaments, Ecclesiastical Vessels, insignia and medals made to order; and a wide variety of tablewares—in silver or plated as desired by clients.

In 1878 a move was made to 21 Hunter Street, where watchmaking and jewellery were included. This address continued up to 1887, but the following year, the premises were at 116 Old South Head Road, Woollahra. In 1894 the number is stated as "120", and the firm of "McLean and Son" ceased to exist in 1896—the premises being taken by another party. There is no indication that any family member was connected with the silversmithing or jewellery trade after this date.   **M.G.**

46 Two fine heavy Ciboria from St. Mary's Cathedral, of standard form one inscribed "St. Mary's Cathedral, Sydney" the other "Presented to the Cathedral by the Members of St. Mary's Christian Doctrine Confraternity, May 24th, 1879".

> *MAKER: J. McLean. WEIGHT: 34 ozs. and 28 ozs. HEIGHT: 29 cm.*
> *CIRCA: 1879 COLLECTION: St. Mary's Cathedral, Sydney.*
> *ILLUSTRATED*

HARDY BROS. LTD.

On 31st March, 1853, John Hardy, aged 22, sailed from London in the ship "Plantagenet" for Australia. He had just completed a partnership agreement with his elder brother Samuel who was a watchmaker and jeweller with shops in St. Ives and Huntington, seventy miles from London.

In August, 1853, John arrived in Sydney and commenced business in Jamieson Street. Flourishing wool and gold trades stimulated demand for quality merchandise and in 1855 he moved to more spacious accommodation in Hunter Street. By 1892 a branch had been established in Brisbane, and in 1907 the partnership of Hardy Bros. was converted to a public company. Ten years later a shop was opened at 298 Collins Street, Melbourne, a few doors away from the present premises built in 1934.

In 1929 the firm had the honour conferred on it of being appointed goldsmiths and jewellers to His Majesty King George V by Royal Warrant from Buckingham Palace, entitling them to the use of the Royal Arms in connection with their business.   **F.N.H.**

Item 46

WILLIAM KERR (1839-1896)

KERR, William born in Londonderry, Northern Ireland in 1839 came to Australia as a young man in the early 1860's, the exact date is unknown, and had a small shop in Wharf Road, Balmain in 1875. He moved to larger premises at 574 George Street in 1876, the shop remaining the same, the number changing to 542-544 George Street, circa 1890. The business continuing there until 1938.

Kerr married Sarah Thornton, circa 1863, and they had seven children, three of whom, William, Walter and Harry, entered the business. Their father dying in 1896 aged 57 years and they carried on the business until 1938 when the property in George Street was sold. The eldest son, William, died aged 90 in 1954, Walter in 1953 aged 82 and Harry in the same year aged 74. For this information I am indebted to Mrs N. Dekyvere.

From the surviving examples of their work, William Kerr Snr. had an inventive turn of mind and many pieces are of extremely original design, even though to current taste incongruous. He was commended for his work in the Sydney International Exhibition in 1879 for jewellery and works of art in silver, both for their tasteful design and good construction.   **J.B.H.**

47 A fine and rare cricketing trophy depicting a cricket match of two batsmen, two umpires and ten players. Mounted with an emu egg to the left and right of the pitch, each egg surmounted by a finial of two cricket bats leaning against a tapered etched glass comport. To the rear a tall palm tree supports a large cut-glass etched dish with fluted etched comport to the top.

MAKER: W. Kerr, Sydney. HEIGHT: 74 cm. CIRCA: 1875
COLLECTION: Museum of Applied Arts & Sciences, Sydney.
ILLUSTRATED

48 A good, large presentation centrepiece, the triform base decorated with a large cast emu, blackened silver swan and lyre bird with gold tail in palm fronds. The glass epergne supported by a stylised palm tree to support the elaborate cut glass bowl.
Inscription: "Presented to the Right Worshipful the Mayor, C. J. Roberts, Esq., J.P., by the Citizens of Sydney, 1879".

MAKER: W. Kerr, Sydney. WEIGHT: 92 ozs. HEIGHT: 54 cm.
CIRCA: 1875 COLLECTION: The Sydney Town Hall.
ILLUSTRATED

49 An attractive four vase epergne, the circular base mounted with blackened silver aboriginal carrying boomerang and gold shield and blackened silver swan amidst various types of ferns. The centre stem dividing into four branches carrying acid etched glass fluted vases. This is part of the presentation plate to Mayor C. J. Roberts, J.P.

MAKER: W. Kerr, Sydney. WEIGHT: 49 ozs. OVERALL Height: 52 cm.
CIRCA: 1875 COLLECTION: The Sydney Town Hall

Item 47

Item 48

50 Good, large presentation centrepiece on three cast feet depicting the Australian Coat of Arms to a rocky base decorated with a kangaroo, a blackened silver swan and a large rock opal, enveloped in a large palm tree. The centre pedestal branching into three parts containing a cut glass epergne.
This is part of the presentation plate to Mayor C. J. Roberts, J.P.

MAKER: W. Kerr, Sydney. SILVER WEIGHT, less opal: 115 ozs. HEIGHT: 58 cm. CIRCA: 1875 COLLECTION: The Sydney Town Hall, by courtesy of The Rt. Hon. The Lord Mayor.

NB: The above centrepieces have been made at different dates and put together for the purposes of presentation as they are not en suite.

51 A good presentation piece of three mounted emu eggs, the one to the left with an emu finial, the one to the right with a kangaroo finial, the one in the centre with a typical Kerr blackened aboriginal carrying a boomerang. The base decorated with snakes and lizards and natural Australia flora and fauna.

MAKER: W. Kerr, Sydney. OVERALL WEIGHT: 42 ozs. MAXIMUM WIDTH: 27 cm. MAXIMUM HEIGHT: 28 cm. CIRCA: 1880 COLLECTION: Mr & Mrs J. D. Altmann, Melbourne.

52 A fine and unusual presentation miniature cradle in silver inscribed "Presented by the Aldermen of the City of Sydney to John Harris Esq., Mayor, on the birth of his daughter, Beatrice Alexandra Victoria, 1881.", mounted on a fine myall wood stand.

MAKER: W. Kerr, Sydney. HEIGHT: 30 cm. WIDTH: 33 cm. CIRCA: 1881 COLLECTION: Mrs H. E. H. Atkinson.

53 A fine and rare gold mounted foundation trowel and mallet for laying the foundation stone of the Great Hall of Sydney Town Hall, 1883, inscribed "Presented by the Aldermen of the City of Sydney to the Mayoress Mrs John Harris on the occasion of the laying the foundation stone of the Great Hall of the Town Hall of Sydney, 13th November, 1883."

MAKER: W. Kerr, Sydney. WEIGHT: 10 ozs. LENGTH: 35 cm. CIRCA: 1883 COLLECTION: Mrs H. E. H. Atkinson.

JOHN H. EAVES

EAVES, John H., one of the late 19th century watchmakers and jewellers of Sydney, is likely to have been connected with the family of that name in the building trade from the 1850's; and he is interesting as a suburban, rather than a city businessman.

In 1881 he was living (and possibly working), in Davy Street, near Darlinghurst. This was a small street, which ran between Riley and Crown Streets, and it contained houses—not all completed or occupied. John Eaves may have "worked for wages" for the next year or so, and then been in partnership as a produce merchant: but he was not in the watchmaking and jewellery trade on his own account.

He is next noted in business as: "J. H. Eaves and Co., watchmakers and jewellers", at 102 Regent Street, Redfern. This arrangement was made about the end of 1885; and it is not known who the "Co." was—it may have been only of a financial nature. Regent Street had mixed shops, and this address was retained for another year, and a branch shop opened on The Corso, Manly.

In 1888 the Redfern premises were abandoned, and John H. Eaves moved to 287 George Street, in the city; while still keeping the Manly shop.

Silver bearing Eaves' name could have been made at Redfern, the city proper, or Manly: though the first two places (dating between about 1885 and 1888), may be more likely. Pieces may even belong to Eaves' "city period"; in which case, there cannot be many of them.

Within another year, the city shop was given up: and from this point, the home and business interests of John H. Eaves are firmly located in Manly. He used his own name, without the "Co.".

In 1892 Eaves was the proprietor of the "Camera Obscura"; a popular tourist attraction on Manly Pier, where he now also had his jewellery and watchmaking business. (A Mrs Eaves ran the Pier refreshment rooms; but the exact relationship is unknown).

During the remainder of the 1890's, John H. Eaves continued at his Manly Pier address, and was living at Manly into the 20th century; though not it seems, actively concerned with a jewellery and watchmaking business.   **M.G.**

54   An unusual sugar basin signed in full "J. H. Eaves, Sydney", but with no other marks. Of extremely plain shape.

MAKER: J. H. Eaves, Sydney. WEIGHT: 8 ozs. WIDTH: 12 cm. HEIGHT: 6 cm. Circa: 1890 Private Collection, Sydney.

W. J. PROUD (1871-1931)

PROUD, William James the founder of the present firm of Prouds Pty. Ltd., was born at Glebe, Sydney, in 1871. The family moved to Paddington, where William grew up; and where his father Thomas John Proud was a builder.

William did not follow his father's business; but after a trip to sea in his youth, settled in Sydney and became involved in the jewellery trade. In 1904 he was able to buy the business of A. E. Goldstein, who traded as: "The Modern Art Jewellery Co.", at 187 Pitt Street, Sydney. The business was then that of: "W. J. Proud, Gem Merchant, Jeweller and Watchmaker". In 1912 the address was the same, but two brothers of William Proud (E. I. and G. D.), had joined him as: "Prouds Ltd.".

In 1917 there were three city addresses, as well as the workshop in Clarence Street, and the firm was also dealing in scientific instruments.

The familiar position on the corner of Pitt and King Streets was occupied by 1921, and became the only city showroom address of the company.

About 1925 Prouds Ltd. placed on the market their own make of sterling quality silverware. As there was no Australian system of hall-marking, the usual course adopted by the few Australian silversmiths who wished to use their own mark, was to have this accepted as a "Registered Trade Mark". In this way such mark became their own property and could be legally used on silverwares manufactured. (These marks of the 20th century are not accurately described as "Hall Marks"; but might be considered the Australian equivalent.)

Prouds Ltd. used a bird as their mark—adding "PROUD", and ".925"; the numeral indicating the standard of 925 parts pure in 1000. On larger pieces, "STERLING SILVER" might also be added, but flatwares may not always carry the marks in full—a small spoon has been noted simply marked: "PROUD/.925/STG.".

A few thousand pounds worth of this range of silverware was sold, but the response was perhaps not encouraging, and about 1928 it was discontinued. To the collector and student of Australian silversmithing, the wares made by Prouds Ltd., during this short period cannot fail to be of interest.

In March, 1931, William James Proud, the founder and managing director of the company, died at his home at Wentworth Falls, N.S.W. The firm continued as a family concern. In 1948 Prouds Pty became a public company.

In February, 1951, Prouds combined with the jewellery firm of Edments; gradually extending to interstate branches. Presently Prouds Pty. Ltd., have eleven stores; including one at Norfolk Island.   **M.G.**

---

55   The Sydney to Hobart Yacht Race Trophy. This fine trophy was designed by Mr W. J. Proud and made by Mr John Priora for Sir Walter Marks, Circa 1912 as a presentation piece to be awarded to the winner of a proposed yacht race between Sydney and Auckland. However the First World War intervened and the race was never run, and the trophy remained in the possession of Prouds until purchased by the George Adams Estate in 1946 for the proposed Sydney to Hobart yacht race and presented to the Cruising Yacht Club of Australia, Sydney.

MAKER: J. Priora. DESIGNER: W. J. Proud. WEIGHT: 288 ozs.
HEIGHT: including plinth 63 cms. CIRCA: 1912
COLLECTION: The Cruising Yacht Club of Australia.
ILLUSTRATED

Item 55

UNASCRIBED NEW SOUTH WALES

56   A most unusual cast silver tray. The base and border cast separately and soldered together. The floral border cast in heavy relief and turned out to the reverse. The centre well engraved and inscribed. I am sure that the silver content of this tray would not qualify it to be sterling silver standard.
Inscription: "Presented to Captain Ninian Miller, Commander of the ship of Wilmot, by the passengers in the year 1842."

   MAKER: No marks. WEIGHT: 85 ozs. DIAMETER: 38 cm.
   CIRCA: 1840 Private Collection, Sydney.

57   A fine heavy set of four Communion Chalices raised from the flat and made to match a pair of old Sheffield Plate Chalices, the originals dated 1848 in St. Stephen's Church, Sydney.

   MAKER: W. J. McD. WEIGHT: 24 ozs. (each). HEIGHT: 22 cm.
   CIRCA: 1860 COLLECTION: St. Stephen's Church, Sydney.

SOUTH AUSTRALIAN SILVERSMITHS

JOHN HENRY PACE

PACE, John Henry. In The Adelaide Examiner, 14th December, 1842; "John Henry Pace, Watch, Clockmaker, Jeweller, No. 3 Rundle Street informs the public that he has commenced in the above line having been all his life in the practical part with the advantages of some years resident in London. Old Gold, Silver bought or taken in exchange."

The Adelaide Observer, 2nd December, 1843; "receives variety of goods ex "Corsair" direct from London."

The Adelaide Observer, 23rd November, 1844; "Mr Pace has just set some pieces of carbonate of copper (from Kapunda Mines) which is well adapted for jewellery etc."

The Adelaide Observer, 28th April, 1847; "J. H. Pace begs to call the attention of the Public to the latest arrivals. Tea and coffee services, dishes and covers, tureens, wine coolers, gold and silver watches (see introduction).

The Adelaide Observer, 13th January, 1849; "J. H. Pace having removed from Rundle to King William Street."

The Adelaide Observer, 5th May, 1849, news item; "Mr Pace burgled of safe with 60 watches, value £300 upwards. Mr Pace was at his residence in the country."

The Adelaide Observer, December, 1849; "Reduction in prices. Only watches and clocks repaired—no silver or jewellery."

J. H. Pace's business opened in 1842 and he appears to have retired to the country by 1849, the business then being run as a clock and watch business.   **J.B.H.**

58   An extremely rare christening mug of standard form. From the inscription and the mark, it may definitely be ascertained that this is, to date, the only surviving piece of South Australian silver pre 1850.
Inscription: "A parting gift to James Miller from his father, 18th May, 1847, South Australia".

MAKER: John Henry Pace, Adelaide. WEIGHT: 4 ozs. HEIGHT: 17 cm.
CIRCA: 1847 COLLECTION: Silver Lyon Ltd., Scotland.
ILLUSTRATED

NB: For this date, one cannot expect a "grand" piece, as the young colony (established December 1836), had suffered a serious depression and decline in population. This has been corrected by the rigorous economies effected by Governor Grey (1841-45), and by 1847 businessmen spoke of the "revival" of the colony.

As the mug was taken to England, it is suggested that the "James Miller" to whom it was originally given, may be identified in the following extract—

"Adelaide (1847)—Shipping Intelligence ". . . Cleared Out Thursday, May 20—The barque "Phoebe", Dale master, for Cape of Good Hope and London. Passengers: Mrs Miller, female servant, and child . . ."" (Eight other Cabin passengers.)

Item 58

JULIUS SCHOMBERG

SCHOMBERG, Julius has proved very difficult to research and I have come across only two references to him in contemporary literature. He collaborated with Firnhaber in the production of the Hanson Cup and is known to have exhibited in the international exhibition in London in 1862 and was awarded a medal for a group in silver.

59 A fine and interesting frosted silver mounted bronze medallion won at the Great Exhibition, London 1851 by various South Australian wheat growers and subsequently mounted in Adelaide by an unknown silversmith, JS. Attributed, however, to Schomberg who was the only working silversmith in Adelaide with these initials at that date. The whole conception of the mount is both interesting, balanced and well executed. The feet are aboriginal heads, the inscribed plaques in bands of laurel leaves, the finial to the top surmounted by an Australian coat of arms.

MAKER: attributed to J. Schomberg, Adelaide. WEIGHT: 22 ozs. HEIGHT: 26 cm.
MAXIMUM WIDTH: 15 cm. CIRCA: 1860
COLLECTION: National Gallery of South Australia.
ILLUSTRATED

CHARLES EDWARD FIRNHABER (1806-1880)

FIRNHABER, Charles arrived in South Australia from Bremen, Germany on 24th March, 1847 with his wife and two children. Four others were later to be born in Australia. The first recorded advertisement is in The Australian Examiner, 15th August, 1851—"Mr Firnhaber, goldsmith, silversmith and jeweller, Union Street, North Adelaide, reminds his friends that he continues to make and repair articles of gold and silver." The South Australian Almanac 1852— "Firnhaber, manufacturing and surgical dentist, also gold and silversmith, in all its branches, Union Street, Near Kermode Street, North Adelaide." Firnhaber had moved to 123 Hindley Street, Adelaide by 1856, his Union Street shop being listed as his private residence. He frequently advertises in the Almanacs for 1852, 1859, 1860, 1862, 1864, etc. The last reference to Firnhaber in the The Trades Directory of South Australia is 1875 and it would appear that he went back to the North Adelaide business premises/home in that year. He died on 25th July, 1880, aged 74, at Kermode Street, his occupation on the death certificate being given as jeweller.

Only the four items listed below by Firnhaber have so far come to light, all of these are extremely well made and designed and the Hanson presentation piece must rank as one of the finest examples of Australian silver. In my opinion, time will produce the evidence that will prove Firnhaber to be Australia's greatest silversmith.

It may be assumed from his advertisement in the South Australian Almanac for 1852 that he was, in fact, a trained dentist, skilled in dental fillings and surgical work and that he turned his hand to silversmithing. Most of his work is cast rather than beaten, a skill more allied to dental work than the raising of articles from the flat as per silversmithing.   **J.B.H.**

Item 59

60 A fine quality racing trophy, the Royal Exchange Cup. Standing on a loaded base to the lobed embossed body and lid topped by a floral finial, inscribed: "Adelaide Races, 2nd January, 1850. Royal Exchange Cup presented by Mr George Coppin and won by Mr Charles Fisher's High Flyer".

MAKER: C. E. Firnhaber, Adelaide. OVERALL WEIGHT: 38 ozs. HEIGHT: 30 cm. CIRCA: 1850 Private Collection, South Australia.
ILLUSTRATED

61 A fine and rare covered cup engraved with the mottos "Love, Friendship, Truth". Silver gilt finial with a hand protruding with a gold heart in the palm.
Inscription: "Loyal Adelaide Lodge 3014 F.M.U. presented as a token of respect to P. G. George Mayo as a surgeon of the above Lodge for his past services, Adelaide January 13, 1851".

MAKER: C. E. Firnhaber, Adelaide. WEIGHT: 28 ozs. HEIGHT: 27 cm. WIDTH: 10½ cm. CIRCA: 1850 COLLECTION: National Galley of South Australia.

62 A fine lidded emu egg cup on a circular base, mounted with simulated Druid weapons joined by a python clasp, the emu egg banded with grape vines with hanging bunches of grapes, the lidded top with an acorn finial. The shield to either side beautifully engraved, one with traditional symbols, the other with presentation inscription: "Presented by the United Ancient Order of Druids to Llandaff Brisbane Matthews by the Order in South Australia, Adelaide, 16th July, 1863".

MAKER: C. E. Firnhaber, Adelaide. WEIGHT: 12 ozs. HEIGHT: 28 cm. CIRCA: 1863 COLLECTION: J. B. Hawkins Antiques.

63 The Hanson Cup. An extremely fine, rare and large Gothic covered cup, fully marked base, body, lid and finial by Charles Edward Firnhaber. The following quotation is taken from the South Australian Advertiser, Monday, July 14th, 1862—
"This cup was designed by Mr Julius Schomberg who also took part in the construction. The principal workman, however, was Mr C. E. Firnhaber. The cup is pure Gothic in its design and on the pedestal are four shields displaying the arms of the Hanson family beautifully chased and surmounted by the crest, a merlin on a cap of maintenance. Below the shield and on a scroll is the motto "Auspice deo nil desperandum". The cup is of polished silver and silver gilt inside. The Gothic open work in frosted silver is most elaborately worked. The cover of the cup is surmounted by a classical figure of Justice blindfolded with sword and scales. The figure is solid silver and four inches high. It is considered by competent judges to be equal to anything turned out by Messrs. Hunt and Roskell. The engraving of the inscription was the work of Mr Payne of King William Street."

MAKER: Charles Edward Firnhaber, Adelaide. WEIGHT: 113 ozs. HEIGHT: 54 cm. CIRCA: 1861 COLLECTION: Dr and Mrs L. Warnock.
ILLUSTRATED

Sir Richard Davies Hanson, 1805-1876, one of the founders of South Australia, arriving that colony 1846, drafted its Constitution 1851-1856 and was Chief Justice of South Australia from 1861-1874. This cup was presented to him on Monday, July 14th 1862 for his services to South Australia. See *Dictionary of Australian Biography*, P. Searle.

Item 60

Item 63

Item 63 (detail)

HENRY STEINER

STEINER, Henry probably arrived in South Australia on 4th February, 1858 on the "Ohio" from Bremen, Germany. He is first listed in the South Australian Almanac for 1864. It is possible, however, that he had opened his business in 1860 and may well have worked for Firnhaber on his arrival as they both came from the same port in Germany and may have known each other in that country. His business premises were always in the one place on the east corner of Rundle Street and Charles Street. The number initially being 108A, it was, however. changed in 1866 to 106A. August L. Brunkhorst, (q.v.) worked for him.

Steiner exhibited at the Inter Colonial Exhibition of Australasia, Melbourne, 1866-1867, the Melbourne International Exhibition for 1880-1881 (q.v.) item 91, also the Paris exhibition in conjunction with Wendt in 1878.

An outbreak of typhoid in 1883 badly affected his family, his wife and two children dying. He appears to have ceased business, possibly as a result of this in 1884, having sold his business to his former employee, Brunkhorst. Through the Register of Deaths, it has been ascertained that Steiner did not die in South Australia and it may be assumed that with the death of his immediate family in 1883, he returned to Germany.

Steiner is amongst the most prolific of all Australian silversmiths. His work varies greatly in standard, some items being very good and some being very bad. His early work is simple and poorly made. His later efforts are flamboyant, peculiarly Australian in their motif and decoration, and on some occasions, he shows outstanding ability, (q.v.) ostrich egg tankard.

J.B.H.

64   Silver mounted emu egg trophy, the earliest surviving dated example of Steiner's work so far located, with applied shield for the inscription, reading: "Presented to Captain G. Mayo from the members of his company as a token of esteem, Adelaide, June 20, 1861".

   MAKER: H. Steiner, Adelaide. WEIGHT: 8 ozs. OVERALL HEIGHT: 20½ cm. WIDTH: 9½ cm. CIRCA: 1860 COLLECTION: National Gallery of South Australia.

64a   A good early presentation trophy on six sided lobed base, the stem of bull-rushes and water lilies supporting the pear shaped bowl. Inscribed: "Presented to George Strickland Kingston Esq. M.P. by the Committee of the S.A. Rifle Association in token of their appreciation of his exertions in 1861 as Hon. Secretary of the Society."

   MAKER: H. Steiner, Adelaide. WEIGHT: 14 ozs. HEIGHT: 29½ cm. WIDTH: 17 cm. CIRCA: 1860 Private Collection, Sydney.

65   An early emu egg decorative ornament of simple form and outline with Steiner's early marks.

   MAKER: H. Steiner, Adelaide. WEIGHT: 10 ozs. HEIGHT: 27 cm. WIDTH: 10 cm. CIRCA: 1860 COLLECTION: J. Klinger, Esq., Adelaide.

66   Emu egg trophy with ring handles surmounted by an eagle with wings extended. On oval embossed rocky base with palm tree support.

   MAKER: H. Steiner, Adelaide. WEIGHT: 8 ozs. HEIGHT: 25 cm. CIRCA: 1860 COLLECTION: F. McDonald, Esq., Sydney.

67   Interesting early Steiner trophy, an emu egg mounted on two wallaby feet, fitted as a candle-stick. A kangaroo finial acting as snuffer.

   MAKER: H. Steiner, Adelaide. OVERALL HEIGHT: 24 cm.
   CIRCA: 1865 Private Collection, Adelaide.

68   Silver ink stand, fitted with two cut glass inkwells with embossed rocky scenes to the lids.

   MAKER: H. Steiner, Adelaide. CIRCA: 1865 Private Collection, Adelaide.

69   A fine standing jewel box (?) formed out of emu egg. The base comprising the cast figures of an emu and a kangaroo, the stem made up of pressed vine leafs and tendril decoration with a cast emu finial. This unusual conception is a purely decorative emu egg and must represent a standard to which other emu eggs must be compared.

   MAKER: H. Steiner of Adelaide. OVERALL WEIGHT: 16 ozs.
   OVERALL HEIGHT: 29 cm. CIRCA: 1865
   COLLECTION: Mr & Mrs J. D. Altmann, Melbourne.

70   A fine and rare cast silver figure of an aboriginal in the form of a candlestick, wearing a possum skin which means he came from the Murray River region. This item is unique in Australian silver as it is the only recorded cast silver candlestick.

   MAKER: H. Steiner, Adelaide. WEIGHT: 17 ozs. HEIGHT: 23 cm.
   CIRCA: 1865 Private Collection, Victoria.

71   A fine heavy emu egg cup and cover. The aboriginal holding the egg up is similar to the Steiner candlestick. This piece is smaller than Item 69 but weighs more. The embossed rocky base applied with cast figures of an emu and kangaroo on which is an aboriginal in cast silver supporting the silver mounted emu egg.

   MAKER: H. Steiner, Adelaide. WEIGHT: 19 ozs. HEIGHT: 29 cm.
   CIRCA: 1865 COLLECTION: Mr & Mrs J. D. Altmann, Melbourne.

72   Pair of silver mounted emu eggs in the form of vases, engraved decoration, cast handles.

   MAKER: H. Steiner, Adelaide. WEIGHT: 10 ozs. each. OVERALL HEIGHT: 30 cm.
   CIRCA: 1865 COLLECTION: Mr & Mrs J. D. Altmann, Melbourne.

73   A very fine and unusual presentation trophy inscribed "Hamley Gun Club 1873 Champion Cup Won by J. W. Blakewell, 15th March, 1874.", surmounted by a figure of a cupid carrying a furled standard. This may have been exhibited in 1865. See Marks Index.

   MAKER: H. Steiner, Adelaide. Weight: 27 ozs. HEIGHT: 39 cm.
   CIRCA: 1865 Private Collection, Victoria.
   ILLUSTRATED

Item 73

74   A good coursing trophy with cast figure of greyhound as the finial, to a silver gilt interior. This is considerably earlier than the inscription.
Inscription: "South Australian Coursing Club St. Leger Trophy, 1883".

MAKER: H. Steiner, Adelaide. WEIGHT: 35 ozs. OVERALL HEIGHT: 32 cm.
WIDTH: 12 cm. CIRCA: 1870 COLLECTION: Mr & Mrs J. D. Altmann, Melbourne.

75   Christening mug initialled "WRF from Grandmama 1875" in engraved border.

MAKER: H. Steiner, Adelaide. WEIGHT: 5 ozs. HEIGHT: 7 cm.
CIRCA: 1875 Private Collection, Adelaide.

76   A good trowel in its original cedar box. Fitted with peacock mother of pearl handle, a silver rope twist junction from the handle to the blade, covered over with laurel leaves and engraved: "Presented to Mrs J. F. Sabine on the occasion of her laying the foundation stone of St. Johns Church, Laura, 16th August, 1875".

MAKER: H. Steiner, Adelaide. WEIGHT: 5 ozs. MAXIMUM LENGTH: 34 cm.
CIRCA: 1875 COLLECTION: National Gallery of South Australia.

77   A fine and unusual emu egg mounted silver claret jug. The finial an emu, the handle a crocodile, well engraved with applied pressed collar to the neck.

MAKER: H. Steiner, Adelaide. OVERALL WEIGHT: 16 ozs. HEIGHT: 28 cm.
CIRCA: 1875 COLLECTION: Mr & Mrs J. D. Altmann, Melbourne.
ILLUSTRATED

78   An interesting pair of carved emu eggs silver mounted, marked Sterling silver, a crown and a lion in one punch. Surmounted by finials of cast silver emus on ebonised plinth. The carving is interesting in that it is in reverse to the normal, the raised decoration of the egg being left in relief so as to cut the figures and decoration from the background.

MAKER: Attributed Steiner, Adelaide. OVERALL WEIGHT: 14 ozs. each.
HEIGHT: 27 cm. CIRCA: 1875 COLLECTION: Mr & Mrs J. D. Altmann, Melbourne

79   A fine and rare silver mounted emu egg perfume bottle holder, the bottles being replacements. The scene on the base comprises a colourful aboriginal scene of three aboriginal figures. The handles to each half of the egg comprising cornucopia full of wheat and fruit. The egg opens by pressing the finial of an aboriginal on top in a downward direction. This conception is duplicated in Edwards' work, who invented it at this stage is not quite clear.

MAKER: H. Steiner, Adelaide. WEIGHT: 30 ozs. HEIGHT: 32 cm.
LENGTH: Open 18 cm. CIRCA: 1875 COLLECTION: B. Caillard, Esq., Victoria.

Item 77

80 A fine and rare perfume bottle holder similar to the previous example, however, it contains its original Queensland bean silver mounted scent bottles and is mounted with an alert figure of a kangaroo as the finial for opening.

MAKER: H. Steiner, Adelaide. WEIGHT: 33 oz. HEIGHT: 35 cm.
CIRCA: 1875 Tamworth City Council, Regan Collection.

81 A fine large silver gilt communion chalice, the only recorded religious vessel by this maker so far noted.

MAKER: H. Steiner, Adelaide. WEIGHT: 12 ozs. HEIGHT: 22 cm. WIDTH: 14 cm.
CIRCA: 1875 COLLECTION: J. Klinger, Esq., Adelaide.

82 Engraved christening mug, initialled MET 1881.

MAKER: H. Steiner, Adelaide. WEIGHT: 6 ozs. HEIGHT: 8 cm.
CIRCA: 1880 Private Collection, Adelaide.

83 A fine large epergne on turned cedar base. The frosted cut glass bowl supported in palm fronds raised on two intertwined palm trunks.

MAKER: H. Steiner, Adelaide. HEIGHT: 47 cm. MAXIMUM WIDTH: 30 cm.
CIRCA: 1880 Private Collection, Adelaide.

84 An epergne standing on six feet, pierced and embossed to a central fluted Chippendale style pillar with applied floral leaves to support the frosted glass bowl. Marked on the base.

MAKER: H. Steiner, Adelaide. WEIGHT: 38 ozs. HEIGHT: 48 cm.
CIRCA: 1880 Collection: Mr & Mrs J. D. Altmann, Melbourne.

85 A fine large epergne on turned cedar base with beautifully cut frosted glass bowl to the top. Supported by intertwined palm trunks amidst falling palm leaves.

MAKER: H. Steiner, Adelaide. WEIGHT: 41 ozs. HEIGHT: 46 cm.
CIRCA: 1880 COLLECTION: J. Patience, Esq., Sydney.

86 A fine large standing table centre piece in the form of an epergne. Two stylised entwined palm trunks supporting a frosted glass bowl, the whole standing on three splayed feet.

MAKER: H. Steiner, Adelaide. OVERALL WEIGHT: 105 ozs. HEIGHT: 58 cm.
WIDTH: 31 cm. CIRCA: 1880 By Courtesy of Her Excellency Lady Hasluck.

87   Large silver claret jug of rather art nouveau form with unusual scroll handle. No inscription but well engraved with small shields depicting herons to either side. Marked on the neck underneath the lip and marked on the base.

MAKER: H. Steiner of Adelaide. WEIGHT: 34 ozs. HEIGHT: 46 cm.
CIRCA: 1880 COLLECTION: Mr & Mrs J. D. Altmann, Melbourne.

88   Cream jug. Crested, heavily engraved and good weight.

MAKER: H. Steiner, Adelaide. WEIGHT: 11 ozs. HEIGHT: 13½ cm. WIDTH: 16 cm.
CIRCA: 1880 Private Collection, Adelaide.

89   Goblet of good gauge and heavy weight and well made with applied embossed fern leaf decoration.
Presentation Inscription for 1880: "For a Ploughing Match" with well engraved period plough to rear.

MAKER: H. Steiner, Adelaide. WEIGHT: 12 ozs. HEIGHT: 19 cm.
CIRCA: 1880 COLLECTION: Mr & Mrs J. D. Altmann, Melbourne.

90   A good silver goblet.
Inscription: "Strathalbyn Agricultural Society, September 1883, President's Cup".

MAKER: H. Steiner, Adelaide. WEIGHT: 7 ozs. HEIGHT: 20 cm.
CIRCA: 1880 COLLECTION: Mr & Mrs J. D. Altmann, Melbourne.

91   An extremely fine and rare presentation casket.
Inscription: "Presented to George Hamilton, Commissioner of Police, by the Officers and non-commissioned Officers and Constables of the South Australian Police Force, June 1881". The contemporary Newspaper description reads—"This casket, which is of Sterling Silver, was manufactured by Mr H. Steiner of Rundle Street and is 22 inches long, of oblong shape. It is of burnished silver and is inlaid with gilding. On the lid which opens with a hinge is a seated boy holding a Horn of Plenty. The figure forms the finial, where he is seated being represented as rough ground, the border is worked to represent peacock feathers. The sides of the casket are engraved with scrolls and a new description of frosting which has a very pleasing effect. Palm leaves in the ornamentation of the base. The casket is supplied with silver handles and rests upon four massive claws. A shield engraved on the lid is inscribed as above, while the Hamilton Coat of Arms crest and motto is engraved upon the front panel. The casket is a highly finished and handsome work of art and is one of the principal pieces shown by Mr Steiner at the Melbourne exhibition of 1881 and for which he received first prize. It contains the presentation scroll on white satin to Hamilton and again I quote "the work being done in Mr Minchin's best manner".

MAKER: H. Steiner, Adelaide. OVERALL WEIGHT: 148 ozs. LENGTH: 52 cm.
HEIGHT: 33 cm. CIRCA: 1880 COLLECTION: National Gallery of South Australia.
ILLUSTRATED

Item 91

92 Cup and cover, the finial depicting a soldier in uniform of the period.
Inscription: "Royal Victorian Fusiliers. Presented by Dr. James to YP No. 1 Camp,
January 1882".

MAKER: H. Steiner, Adelaide. WEIGHT: 9 ozs. OVERALL HEIGHT: 27 cm.
CIRCA: 1882 Private Collection, Melbourne.

93 A fine severe good quality jug, well marked on the neck, the frosted body well engraved
and inscribed: "South Australian Coursing Club, Buckland Park, all aged stakes, 1882
President's Cup presented by R. Barr-Smith".

MAKER: H. Steiner, Adelaide. WEIGHT: 24 ozs. OVERALL HEIGHT: 38 cm.
CIRCA: 1882 Private Collection, Adelaide.

94 A fine tall claret jug inscribed "South Australian Coursing St. Ledger Stakes Trophy,
Presented by the Hon. E. T. Smith, 1884".

MAKER: H. Steiner, Adelaide. WEIGHT: 24 ozs. HEIGHT: 42 cm. WIDTH: 19 cm.
CIRCA: 1884 COLLECTION: J. Klinger, Esq., Adelaide.
ILLUSTRATED

95 A fine embossed and engraved claret jug with unusual handle and spout, inscribed "Presented to T. R. Bright Esq., J.P. on his leaving Clare, December 1888." Sold by Brunkhorst
who purchased Steiner's shop 1884.

MAKER: H. Steiner, Adelaide. WEIGHT: 20 ozs. HEIGHT: 36 cm. WIDTH: 11 cm.
CIRCA: 1884 Private Collection, Victoria.

96 An extremely fine and rare silver gilt lined ostrich egg, mounted in the form of a tankard
with well cast thumb piece and cast silver base, marked in the base and on the handle. One
of Steiner's last commissions, this highly original tankard owes its origins to 17th Century
German work and is in the best tradition of German immigrant silversmiths working with
local materials in South Australia.

MAKER: H. Steiner, Adelaide. WEIGHT: 25 ozs. HEIGHT: 18 cm.
MAXIMUM WIDTH: 17 cm. CIRCA: 1884 Private Collection, Victoria.
ILLUSTRATED

97 A fine two handled presentation trophy of the best Sterling content with fluted and ribbed
handles, the whole raised from the flat. Applied strapwork decoration to the base of the
bowl.
Inscription: "South Australian Coursing Club Waterloo Cup for 1886, a gift of the President, M. R. Barr-Smith, won by Mr Handel Allen's Violet out of King of the Hills."

MAKER: H. Steiner, Adelaide. WEIGHT: 40 ozs. CIRCA: 1880
COLLECTION: Mr & Mrs J. D. Altmann, Melbourne.

NB: This must have been left over stock already marked by Steiner but engraved and sold by Brunkhorst.

Item 94

Item 96

98 An English silver teapot, overstamped with Steiner's marks and fitted with a kangaroo finial. Inscribed and dated 1884, the last year of Steiner's business. It may be assumed that this was a last minute order and comprises part of a tea service. To fill the order, Steiner took an English tea service and over-punched it. Martin Hall & Co. were the original makers.

MAKERS MARK Now: H. Steiner, Adelaide. WEIGHT: 24 ozs. HEIGHT: 16 cm. WIDTH: 26 cm. CIRCA: 1870 English. COLLECTION: National Gallery of South Australia.

JOCHIM MATTHIAS WENDT (1830-1917)

WENDT, Jochim Matthias, born in 1830 in the village of Dageling near the town of Itzehoe in the province of Schleswig-Holstein in Denmark. He completed his education by being apprenticed to the village watchmaker and learning the trades of watchmaker and silversmith. He decided to emigrate to South Australia in 1854, opening his first shop in Pirie Street. His fine natural ability based on a good training and delicate craftsmanship led him to be in great demand. The business soon outgrew these premises and he moved to Rundle Street. He opened extensions to the business in 1871 at Mount Gambier and had another branch at Broken Hill, this branch being the first stone building in the town. Both branches have long since closed.

In 1872 he married Johanna Coeppen, a widow with four children whose husband had died in 1868. The eldest son, Herman Coeppen, went into partnership with Wendt and added the surname Wendt to his own. In 1880, the Adelaide shop moved to 70 Rundle Street, this number was later changed to become 76 and finally 74. All these numbers, however, refer to the same shop. In the 1890's Wendt turned to other fields of investment and was a major shareholder in the syndicate which erected the Theatre Royal in Hindley Street, the Adelaide Arcade, the largest building of its type in Australia when built, and the Free Masons Hall in Flinders Street, In 1904 the premises had been outgrown so completely that they had to be rebuilt and arcade type walls were installed in 1915. In 1917 Wendt died, aged 87 and his stepson, H. K. Wendt, took over the business.

Major recorded items by this maker:

1864-1865: Wendt took first prize at the Dunedin exhibition in New Zealand—see illustration K. Albrecht (lost).

1867: The Duke of Edinburgh visited Adelaide and Wendt made a piece of silver as a presentation piece from the colonists. By this time he had 12 silversmiths employed in the business and was importing pressed moulding from abroad.

1867: He made four magnificent silver caskets with Australian motifs for the Duke of Edinburgh who was so delighted that he commissioned a further 400 guineas worth to be despatched to Queen Victoria. As a consequence, Wendt was appointed official jeweller to his Royal Highness the Duke of Edinburgh in the Colony of South Australia and the Royal Coat of Arms was erected outside the shop.

1878: Wendt was awarded two first prizes for silverware at the 1878 Paris exhibition, his goods being displayed in a cabinet with Steiner (q.v.). The pair of silver epergnes were purchased at the exhibition and presented to the British Commissioner, Sir Phillip Cunliffe-Owen.

1901: The Commonwealth of Australia came into being, the first parliament was opened by H.R.H. the Duke of Cornwall, later King George V, who was presented with a casket made by Wendt, featuring bush scenes and an aboriginal stalking a kangaroo. Also in that year he made a model of the Block Ten Mine commissioned by the directors as a presentation to their manager, Mr J. M. Warren. This model shows in detail the slag heaps and surface works, the pit propping and modes of operation of that mine, in the most remarkable detail. (lost) For further information see privately printed history of Wendt family business. From which the above is extracted.

J.B.H.

99   A fine and rare candle holder and snuffer, with beaded border to a perfectly plain body, original snuffer and sconce.

   MAKER: J. M. Wendt, Adelaide. WEIGHT: 10 ozs. HEIGHT: 7 cm. WIDTH: 16½ cm. CIRCA: 1870 Private Collection Adelaide.
   ILLUSTRATED

100   A fine inkstand mounted in malachite and black marble with cast applied frosted border to the feet, two cut glass inkwells with cast applied rope twist mounts and oxidised blackened silver aboriginal carrying spear and shield.

   MAKER: J. M. Wendt, Adelaide. MAXIMUM HEIGHT: 23 cm.
   MAXIMUM WIDTH: 28 cm. CIRCA: 1870
   COLLECTION: National Gallery of South Australia.
   ILLUSTRATED

NB: Malachite was mined at Burra Burra in the 1860's and Australian silver with malachite mounts is nearly always by an Adelaide maker.

101   Trowel—"Presented to W. J. Marchant, Esq., on laying the foundation stone of Strathalbyn Institute, June 5, 1874".

   MAKER: J. M. Wendt, Adelaide. LENGTH: 35 cm. WIDTH: 10 cm.
   CIRCA: 1870 COLLECTION: Ramornie Antiques, Sydney.

102   A very fine and rare cast silver seal, inset with South Australian malachite, the intaglio crest of Prior/Pryor/Pryer, of a shell with the initials TP in the base which is decorated with cast applied figures of a lubra, dead kangaroo and aboriginal.

   MAKER: Unknown, possibly Wendt. CIRCA: 1875 Private Collection, Adelaide.

103   A good cup in absolutely pristine original condition, the frosted body with central burnished silver raised plaques inscribed: "Royal Agricultural, Horticultural Society of South Australia" and dated on the other side 1876.

   MAKER: J. M. Wendt, Adelaide. WEIGHT: 21 ozs. OVERALL HEIGHT: 35 cm.
   MAXIMUM WIDTH: 19 cm. CIRCA: 1875
   COLLECTION: National Gallery of South Australia.

Item 99

Presented to Samuel James Way Esq. Q.C.
on his elevation to the Bench, as a token
of esteem by the members of his office
69 King William St.   2nd March 1876

104 A presentation trophy inscribed "O.R.C. Oakbank—Members Steeplechase Won by Mr F. T. Cornelius's "B.G. Rollo", Ridden by the Owner, March 6 1880."

MAKER: J. M. Wendt, Adelaide. WEIGHT: 12½ ozs. HEIGHT: 31 cm.
WIDTH: 10 cm. CIRCA: 1880 Private Collection, Victoria.

105 A silver mounted emu egg candle stick, the base group consisting of three well executed 10 cm high cast silver figures of an aboriginal and two kangaroos. The finial to the top which acts as a snuffer is missing.

MAKER: J. M. Wendt, Adelaide: WEIGHT: 26 ozs. HEIGHT: 19 cm. LENGTH: 28 cm.
CIRCA: 1860 COLLECTION: B. Caillard, Esq., Victoria.

106 A very fine and rare ostrich egg goblet with silver gilt interior, held up by an aboriginal wearing a silver gilt possum's skin, standing on an embossed fern base. The figure is cast.

MAKER: J. M. Wendt, Adelaide. WEIGHT: 24 ozs. HEIGHT: 31 cm. WIDTH: 12 cm.
CIRCA: 1865 Private Collection, Victoria.
ILLUSTRATED

107 A fine and rare silver mounted emu egg ink well with a scene of grazing emus inserted into the egg. The whole surmounted by a silver cockatoo, removable to disclose the ink well.

MAKER: J. M. Wendt, Adelaide. Signature partially erased. WEIGHT: 42 ozs.
HEIGHT: 23 cm. WIDTH: 24 cm. CIRCA: 1870
COLLECTION: B. Caillard, Esq., Victoria.

108 A fine oval salver, the grape vine border cast and applied with tendrils and leaves. The feet, sheafs of corn decoratively fitted into the cast mounts terminating in pawed feet. Inscription: "Presented to S. S. Young, Esq., by a number of his fellow colonists on his leaving Adelaide to assume the general management of the National Bank of Australasia, 29th July, 1870" and his motto is "Be right and persist".

MAKER: J. M. Wendt, Adelaide. WEIGHT: 75 ozs. SIZE: 40 cm x 48 cm.
CIRCA: 1870 Private Collection, Victoria.
ILLUSTRATED

109 A good silver coursing trophy surmounted with well cast finial of a greyhound, all of good gauge and weight. Inscription: "South Australian Coursing Club, St. Leger Trophy, 1882."

MAKER: J. M. Wendt, Adelaide. WEIGHT without base: 39 ozs. HEIGHT: 40 cm.
WIDTH: 20 cm. CIRCA: 1882 COLLECTION: Mr & Mrs J. D. Altmann, Melbourne.

110 A teapot engraved with the motto "Servire deo Sapere" to a fine plain body raised from the flat, fitted with square tapering handle.

MAKER: J. M. Wendt, Adelaide. WEIGHT: 14 ozs. HEIGHT: 11 cm. WIDTH: 20 cm
CIRCA: 1890 Private Collection, Adelaide.

Item 106

Item 108

111 A plain mug with gilt lined interior inscribed on the body "Here's Luck".

> *MAKER: J. M. Wendt, Adelaide. WEIGHT: 10 ozs. HEIGHT: 11 cm.*
> *CIRCA: 1890 Tamworth City Council, Regan Collection.*

112 A fine and rare small three piece tea service with well engraved decoration.

> *TEAPOT—Height: 13 cm. Width: 17 cm.*
> *CREAM JUG—Height: 8 cm. Width: 12 cm.*
> *SUGAR BASIN—Height: 11 cm. Width: 11 cm.*
> *MAKER: J. M. Wendt, Adelaide. CIRCA: 1890 Private Collection, Victoria.*

113 *Foundation trowel* with the inscription "Presented to the Hon. Sir Henry Parkes, G.C.M.G., by the Barrier Colonial District of the A.M.A. of Australasia, April, 4th 1890." With original box the label on the box stating J. M. Wendt, watchmaker, jeweller, silversmith by appointment to H.R.H. Duke of Edinburgh, 70 Rundle Street, Adelaide and Mt. Gambier.

> *MAKER: J. M. Wendt, Adelaide. LENGTH: 30 cm.*
> *CIRCA: 1890 COLLECTION: Mitchell Library, Sydney.*

114 A fine tall ewer of classical design and good weight.

> *MAKER: J. M. Wendt, Adelaide. WEIGHT: 25 ozs. HEIGHT: 39 cm.*
> *CIRCA: 1890 Tamworth City Council, Regan Collection.*

115 A very fine frosted silver presentation trophy with good beaded borders and cast applied handles.
Inscription: "The St. Paul's Lager Bier Vase, 1900-1901".

> *MAKER: J. M. Wendt of Adelaide. WEIGHT: 40 ozs. HEIGHT: 33 cm.*
> *WIDTH: 18 cm. CIRCA: 1900 COLLECTION: Mr & Mrs J. D. Altmann, Melbourne*

116 An extremely fine and rare six piece tea and coffee service, with tray. Engraved with ferns and initialled 'M' and dated 1900. Part frosted and part plain, comprising the kettle on stand, teapot, coffee pot, cream jug, lidded sugar bowl and tray. It was presented as a wedding present to a daughter of Sir Charles Todd, the man who superintended the erection of the overland telegraph line to Alice Springs. With original travelling box.

> *MAKER: J. M. Wendt, Adelaide. OVERALL WEIGHT: 260 ozs.*
> *TRAY: 58 cm x 35 cm. COFFEE POT: Height: 30 cm. CREAM JUG: 17½ cm.*
> *SUGAR BOWL: 20 cm. KETTLE ON STAND: 33 cm. CIRCA: 1900*
> *Private Collection, England.*
> *ILLUSTRATED*

Item 116

AUGUST L. BRUNKHORST (1846-1919)

BRUNKHORST, August arrived in South Australia in 1877 and worked for H. Steiner from 1877-1882 when he set up for himself in business in King William Street. In 1884, H. Steiner retired and Brunkhorst bought the business and moved into Steiner's old premises, taking over his stock and goodwill. The Waterloo Cup for 1886 made by Steiner was sold by Brunkhorst. The premises still at the corner of Rundle Street and Charles Street, changed from 106A to 110 in 1892. In 1918-1919 Brunkhorst also had premises at North Street, Frewville as his premises in Rundle Street were demolished in August or September 1915. Brunkhorst died in 1919, aged 71, unmarried, occupation on death certificate, given as silversmith. The business was taken over by Caris Bros., watchmakers and jewellers, now the site of Coles supermarket.

Brunkhorst's work is very much in the art nouveau style, plain, simple lines with a minimum of ornamentation. The construction is good and the items in general well proportioned. However, he seems to have escaped the tendency for standardisation and his output bears the stamp of individuality. **J.B.H.**

117 Good brandy flask, crested, of full shape, heavy gauge, turned stopper and fitted piano hinge handles. Engraved with crest to front.

MAKER: A. Brunkhorst, Adelaide. WEIGHT: 16 ozs. HEIGHT with handle up: 12 cm. WIDTH: 13 cm. CIRCA: 1890 Private Collection, Adelaide.

118 A good claret jug of semi-art nouveau form with tapering body. This seems to be typical of Adelaide work of this period, the frosted surfaces being used by Wendt and Steiner. Of good heavy gauge.
Inscription: "Adelaide Hunt Club 1898. The Drag Cup presented by G. Downer, Esq."

MAKER: A. Brunkhorst, Adelaide. WEIGHT: 23 ozs. HEIGHT: 34 cm. CIRCA: 1895 Private Collection, Melbourne.
ILLUSTRATED

119 Small stamp box, inscribed "JF, 14th September, 1898".

MAKER: A. Brunkhorst, Adelaide. WEIGHT: $2\frac{1}{2}$ ozs. HEIGHT: 3 cm. WIDTH: 6 cm. CIRCA: 1895 Private Collection, Adelaide.

120 Card box, rectangular shape, fitted interior gilded, crest to the front.

MAKER: A. Brunkhorst, Adelaide. WEIGHT: 5 ozs. HEIGHT: $6\frac{1}{2}$ cm. WIDTH: $9\frac{1}{2}$ cm. CIRCA: 1900 Private Collection, Adelaide.

121 A good small snuff box of plain form.

MAKER: A. Brunkhorst, Adelaide. WEIGHT: 3 ozs. LENGTH: 12 cm. WIDTH: $5\frac{1}{2}$ cm. CIRCA: 1900 COLLECTION: J. Klinger, Esq., Adelaide.

Item 118

122 A good plain hot water jug with beaded border to the lid and base. The crest of Dutton to the front with a well turned finial to the lid.

MAKER: A. Brunkhorst, Adelaide. WEIGHT: 14 ozs. HEIGHT: 26 cm. WIDTH: 15 cm. CIRCA: 1900 Private Collection Adelaide.

123 En suite with the above, cream jug.

MAKER: A. Brunkhorst, Adelaide. WEIGHT: 13 ozs. HEIGHT: 20 cm. WIDTH: 16 cm. CIRCA: 1900 Private Collection, Adelaide.
ILLUSTRATED

124 A good rare four piece silver tea service comprising tray, cream jug, sugar bowl and teapot. Inscription: "Presented to Mr and Mrs J. Darling on the occasion of their silver wedding, 14th October, 1900"

MAKER: A. Brunkhorst, Adelaide. WEIGHT: 46 ozs. TRAY: $29\frac{1}{2}$ cm x 22 cm. CIRCA: 1900 Private Collection, Adelaide.

125 A good trophy, again with a frosted body and very much in the art nouveau style. Inscription: "Royal Agricultural and Horticultural Society of South Australia Incorporated, September 1909, awarded to W. J. Davies."

MAKER: A. Brunkhorst, Adelaide. WEIGHT: 19 ozs. HEIGHT: 30 cm. WIDTH: 15 cm. CIRCA: 1905 Private Collection, Melbourne.

WALTER HUNTER STEVENSON (1855-1930)

STEVENSON, Walter was born in Carlton, Victoria, one of eleven children of Scottish parentage. His father was an official of the Victorian Legislative Council. First employed in a legal firm he later served his apprenticeship with Phillip Wing a silversmith and goldsmith of Little Collins Street, Melbourne. In 1875 he became a journeyman with the firm of Messrs. Falk & Co. of Adelaide. In 1878 he started business on his own account in leased premises in Gawler Place. During that year he married Harriet Elizabeth Brooke an Adelaide girl of English parentage. He soon moved to larger premises and was employing fifteen hands. He sold the manufacturing business and opened a retail jewellery establishment, the genesis of Stevenson Bros. Ltd., with his brother William, a former clergyman, who had been trained as a watchmaker. Premises were obtained at 6 Rundle Street. Larger premises were acquired in Rundle Street and in 1920 the firm was formed into a limited company. Between 1886 and 1887 Stevenson was a member of the city council and was later the President of the Retail Jewellers' Association and Federal President of the Federated Jewellers' Association of Australia. He died at Fitzroy, South Australia in November 1930.   **K.F.**

126 An extremely fine and rare presentation racing trophy, the two handles surmounted by cast horses heads, the finial to the lid a standing figure of a jockey holding a whip (missing). The lid embossed with a racing scene in continuous relief, the body further embossed with floral decoration, on one side a horse, cattle and sheep, to the other an inscribed cartouche.

MAKER: W. Stevenson, Adelaide. WEIGHT: 45 ozs. HEIGHT: 53 cm.
CIRCA: 1885 Tamworth City Council, Regan Collection.

127 Fine and large presentation claret jug with frosted silver body and embossed decoration and hollow, pierced, handle.
Inscription: "Stevenson Challenge Cup presented to the South Australian Cricketing Association by Stevenson Bros. won by the Norwood Cricket Club three years in succession, 1888, 1889 and 1890."

MAKER: Stevenson Bros., Adelaide. WEIGHT: 34 ozs. OVERALL HEIGHT: 45 cm.
CIRCA: 1890 COLLECTION: Mr & Mrs J. D. Altmann, Melbourne.
ILLUSTRATED

128 A fine heavy tray bearing the Dutton crest.

MAKER: Stevenson, Adelaide. WEIGHT: 36 ozs. WIDTH: 33 cm x 24 cm.
CIRCA: 1900 Private Collection, Adelaide.
ILLUSTRATED

Item 127

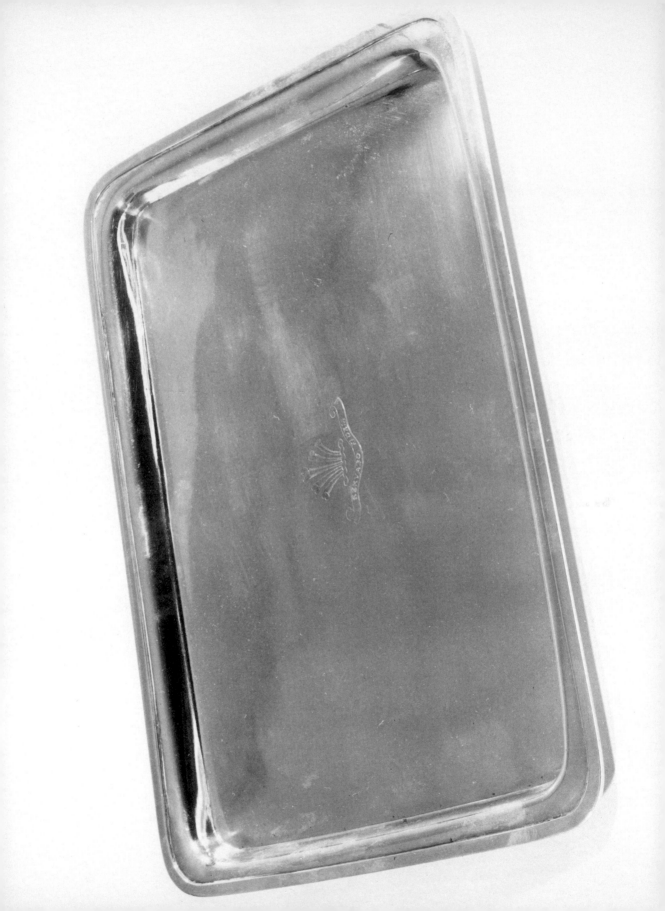

FREDERICK BASSE

BASSE, Frederick, jeweller and art merchant, Church Terrace, Walkerville, Adelaide, carried on business in Rundle Street. He was very successful and had many interests. Born in England, his mother was Swiss and his father French. Always interested in things military he fought on the side of Germany in the Franco Prussian War of 1870. He was appointed staff officer of the 1st Battalion Cadets of South Australia in 1889, and had lodge interests and a number of other honorary positions in civic organisations.   **F.N.H.**

129 Two bowls and a wine taster dimensions and weights not known.

MAKER: F. Basse, Adelaide. CIRCA: 1910 Private Collection, Adelaide.

M. KENDRICK

FIDLER & KENDRICK

KENDRICK, M. design goldsmith, Adelaide, South Australia, produced fine quality silverware, including crescent-shaped and rectangular wine labels.
FIDLER & KENDRICK, manufacturing goldsmiths, Adelaide, produced a fine gold chalice and paten in 1921 for presentation by Roman Catholics of South Australia to Archbishop Spence. Mr Kendrick, snr, was responsible for the major part of the production.
Manufacturing Jewellers Gazette Aug 1920
"As a specimen of ecclesiastical work it has certainly not been surpassed in this country. The style is somewhat Romanesque, though no strong architectural features are involved. Hexagonal feet support a conical bowl. One of the feet has a cross inscribed on it. Each of the six portions of the base is carefully mitred into the adjoining pieces. The decoration of the chalice is based on the grape vine, symbolising the Holy Eucharist, and is adorned with six carbuncles. Surrounding the top of the chalice is engraved in old English type, Hic est enam calix sanguinis. Surrounding the base of the chalice are the words Ex donis Fideluim Archdiocesis Adelaidensis iii, et Rev. Bro. Roberto Guilelmo Spence, Archiepiscopo ejusdem Archdiocesis, 22 Febuarii, 1921. The gold paten bears the symbol IHS in relief. All the ornamentation is in repousse and of the highest excellence, and needless to say, the handiwork of the artisan in gold is exemplified only in this present day."   **F.N.H.**

130 Set of four wine labels, port, sherry, gin, whisky, of rectangular shape with stamped edges and reeded borders, original chains, and another pair with embossed floral borders for whisky and brandy.

MAKER: M. Kendrick, Adelaide. CIRCA: 1910 Private Collection, Melbourne.

VICTORIAN SILVERSMITHS

WILLIAM BENNETT

BENNETT, William, watchmaker, etc., opened his Melbourne business in 1843, and in "The Melbourne Argus" of 16th July, 1847, advertised for a good workman, also taking the opportunity to thank his friends and customers for their very liberal patronage during the past five years. He went to Ballarat in 1860 and the business was carried on until his son died in 1940, after having risen to the rank of Colonel in World War I.

William Bennett's watch and jewellery establishment could have been one of the earliest shops of its kind in Victoria. There may even be a piece or two of his handicraft extant.   **F.N.H.**

CHARLES BENNETT

The following two items are marked respectively in full "Charles Bennett, Melbourne". As it is impossible to locate any reference to Charles Bennett from contemporary newspaper reports or advertisements, I have been unable to give any form of biography, however, on the evidence of the coffee pot and entree dish illustrated, he was a very fine craftsman and designer. He may have been related to William Bennett. His working dates would approximate between 1840 and 1850.   **J.B.H.**

131 The La Trobe Entree Dish. A fine, rare and interesting lidded entree dish and liner with plain reeded handles. Gadroon applied cast borders, all three parts raised from the flat, square piano rule hinge handles, underneath one handle engraved G. J. La Trobe. Crested to the front with a hand emerging from a cloud clutching an anchor and the motto "Quie Cherche trouve" for G. J. La Trobe, marked in full.

> *MAKER: Charles Bennett, Melbourne. WEIGHT: 42 ozs. HEIGHT: 24 cm.*
> *CIRCA: 1845 Private Collection, Victoria.*
> *ILLUSTRATED*

132 An extremely rare and fine coffee pot fitted with percolated liner, large splayed wooden handle. The applied reeded bands to the pot to a straight spout emerging from the base. The idea of percolating coffee in a coffee pot is very much a French idea, since this article was made by the same maker as the La Trobe entree dish, there is a possibility they were made for the same person.

> *MAKER: Charles Bennett, Melbourne, marked underneath the finial in full.*
> *WEIGHT: 38 ozs. HEIGHT: 24 cm. MAXIMUM WIDTH: 30 cm.*
> *CIRCA: 1845 Private Collection, Victoria.*
> *ILLUSTRATED*

Item 131

Item 132

CHARLES BRENTANI

BRENTANI, Charles arrived in Port Phillip, via Launceston, Van Diemen's Land, on 17th November, 1845. The steerage passenger list of the brig "Scout", has his name as: "Charles Brintain"—but mis-spells are commonly found. A check of "Imports" brought in by "Scout", shows that "4 cases, 1 bale slops" had been carried for "Charles Brintain": no doubt stock-in-trade, while "slops" was a general term for clothing.

On 31st October, 1845, also from Launceston, the brig "Swan" had arrived at Port Phillip, and among the steerage passengers was one "Flemming". Although not all goods carried on "Swan" are specified as to owner, the "10 packages looking glasses" and "1 case clocks", makes interesting reading.

An announcement dated 25th November, 1845, stated that: "C. Brentani, from Italy, Barometer, Thermometer, Looking Glass Maker and Gilder . . . having just arrived in Melbourne . . . has taken a shop . . . (in) . . . Collins-street, opposite the Wesleyan Chapel". (This pinpoints Brentani—the Chapel was on the corner of Collins and Queen Streets.)

At the same time, D. H. Fleming advises that "in connection with the above establishment", he too has just opened up in Collins Street as "Watchmaker and Working Jeweller".

It is suggested that this is the "Fleming" referred to as a passenger on "Swan"; and that between the two of them, Messrs. Brentani and Fleming had very smartly set up in business. It may have been typical of Brentani that he says: "Cash Only" for his transactions: it is obvious that he was not "slow" as a businessman.

Within twelve months or so, Brentani was the sole proprietor of the "Watch, Clock and Jewellery Establishment" which he referred to in the Port Phillip Almanack, published 1st January, 1847. He said that he had "engaged both London and Paris workmen"—but whether Mr Fleming was one of these, is not known. The looking glasses seem to have gone: and one might surmise that there was some arrangement with the compatriot Mr Cetta, the Sydney looking glass maker, who was visiting Melbourne in October, 1846. Brentani concentrated on jewellery wares.

Charles (Carlo?) Brentani was a man of varied talents, and emerges as a character in his own right. In October, 1848, the Press noted the silver snuff box he had made for the dashing Mr Sugden (q.v.); but in 1849 Brentani received more Press notice than he probably wished for.

He and a friend had come into possession of pieces of ore, which yeilded 95% pure gold. The story of subterfuge; comings and goings; and subsequent furore created, reads like a comic opera. (Important gold discoveries in Victoria came later.)

Charles Brentani is lost track of after about 1855, and it is possible that he died in this year. Mrs Brentani was living at Eastern Hill in 1857, and in the 1860's at St. Kilda. There is no reason to consider that she was in financial straits—the writer inclines to the belief that perhaps like Charles Brentani, she managed nicely on her own account.   **M.G.**

133 An extremely rare and fine snuff box in original wooden case, the top veneered with various colonial woods and centred with a silver plaque initialled WJS. The box has an applied cast embossed scene of a kangaroo and emu to the lid, and an embossed border to the base, and the snap handle depicting a fox.

Inscription: "Advance Australia. Presented by the licensed victuallers of the City of Melbourne and friends to Mr W. J. Sudgen on his resignation of the office of Chief Constable in testimony of their respect and esteem for the integrity of his character and his upright, manly and honourable conduct during his period of office, and their sincere wishes for his future prosperity and welfare. Melbourne, November 1st, 1848".

MAKER: Charles Brentani, Melbourne. WEIGHT: 14 ozs. HEIGHT: 4 cm.
WIDTH: 14 cm. DEPTH: 8½ cm. CIRCA: 1848 Private Collection, Victoria.
ILLUSTRATED

Mr William Johnson Sugden was a sheriff's officer when he succeeded Mr Brodie as Chief Constable in 1844. Sugden was said to be a tall, handsome man, who had served with a cavalry regiment. For contemporary reference, see Port Phillip Herald, 31 October, 1848—"Mr Brentani has shown us a very handsome silver snuff box of his own manufacture which is about to be presented to Mr Sugden. It weighs no less than 16 ozs. at a cost of 18 guineas." It is interesting to note that the current weight is 14 ozs.

Item 133

ERNEST LEVINY (1818-1905)

LEVINY, Ernest was born at Szepes-Szombat, Hungary, in 1818. A trained silversmith and jeweller by profession he went to Paris in the 1840's, on to England in 1846 from whence he came to Australia in 1853. Trying to exploit the gold rush he brought his own mining equipment and set up in Castlemaine in Victoria. Unsuccessful, he turned to his other skills of silversmithing and jewellery in the Market Square, Castlemaine. He prospered and his youngest daughter by his second marriage still lives at the family home "Buda" in Hunter Street, Castlemaine.

Leviny appears to have made few pieces, all of which are unmarked, but of very high quality if rather ornate; he employed Frederick Kronberg, a Hungarian living in London, who came to Castlemaine in 1855, whose listed occupation was that of jeweller.

Leviny died in Castlemaine having had ten children by his second marriage, for obituary see Mount Alexander Mail, 7th March, 1905.

He exhibited a gold inkstand in the London International Exhibition 1862, for illustration see Art Journal Catalogue, Page 153. (lost)

Two cups and a series of cast silver horses still in the possession of the family.

(Extracted from *The Art Bulletin of Victoria* 1970-1971)   **J.B.H.**

134 An extremely fine and rare centrepiece. A figure of Victory stands above a nugget of gold, holding a laurel wreath in each hand. The four figures at the base represent the personification of Justice, goldmining, farming and the indigenous aboriginal tribes. It suggests the victorious struggle of man in the goldfields and on the land. This piece is unique in that few Australian silversmiths attempted such experiment with allegory.
Inscription: "Presented 31 December, 1863 to Charles Abraham Saint by his friends and fellow citizens in recognition of many services rendered as editor of the Mt. Alexander Mail to the town and district of Castlemaine from September 1851 to December 1863".

MAKER: E. Leviny. WEIGHT: 67 ozs. HEIGHT: 48.6 cm.
MAXIMUM WIDTH: 15.8 cm. CIRCA: 1863
COLLECTION: National Gallery of Victoria.
ILLUSTRATED

Item 134

WILLIAM EDWARDS

EDWARDS, William. Perhaps the most prolific and distinguished colonial Australian gold-smith was William Edwards who arrived in Melbourne aboard the ship "Blanche Moore" in July, 1857 from London.

As a gentleman he travelled in the chief cabin which was reserved for the more well to do or notable. Unfortunately, this denies us the usual personal particulars other than that he was 38 years of age, such passengers were not listed under the general headings provided on the ships' forms, which furnished certain marital, nationality and sometimes more personal information about the immigrants and visitors.

Whatever we lack as to Edwards' background, family, etc. he has made up for us in his work, which is always of high standard and of historic and artistic interest. Edwards got away from the pseudo British hall marks, using EMU WE KANGAROO as his standard marks with hardly any variations.

William Edwards is listed in the Melbourne Directory at 129 Collins Street East in 1859, and variously thereafter as manufacturer of gold and silver plate at 85 Collins Street. At the International Exhibition 1861, Melbourne, (exhibit No. 467) he was one of the Victorian masters winning a First Class Certificate for worked silver, Ernest Leviny being the other.

In 1866-1867 at the International Colonial Exhibition, Melbourne, Edwards won an honourable mention for "good workmanship of epergnes of most tasteful craftsmanship". It has been suggested that shortly afterwards he returned permanently to England disillusioned with the lack of demand for first quality work, however, Edwards took in a partner Circa 1870, Alexander Kaul.

Alexander Kaul was born 1833, arrived in Melbourne from England aboard the ship "Peru" in December, 1852, and was working as a watchmaker at Ballarat either at Bakery or Black Hill by 1856.

Edwards has been found in Melbourne Directories as late as 1878, and he changed his business address from 85 Collins Street East, to 31 Collins Street West, his private residence being given as Albert Road in Emerald Hill. From 1873 to 1888 the firm of William Edwards and A. A. Kaul "manufacturing goldsmiths, silversmiths, jewellers, etc." was listed at 31 Collins Street West. As William Edwards of this partnership lived in Albert Road, Emerald Hill, he was apparently the person referred to in the earlier entries. The firm of Edwards and Kaul was, however, reported as having been established in 1856. This is open to conjecture. In 1888 the partnership moved again to 5 Collins Street West, Melbourne.

> 1859-1860 W. Edwards, 129 Collins Street East.
> 1861 to Circa 1872 W. Edwards, 85 Collins Street.
> 1873-1888 Edwards & Kaul, 31 Collins Street West.
> 1889 Edwards & Kaul, 5 Collins Street West.

The business of Edwards and Kaul may well have been in operation at 31 Collins Street West as a manufacturing silversmiths shop with a retail outlet at 85 Collins Street in the name of William Edwards from Circa 1860. In 1873 Edwards may well have retired from the business, taken his silent partner Kaul into direct partnership and opened a new retail business at 31 Collins Street West. No silver marked with W. Edwards mark appears to have been made after 1870 and no item so far located bears Edwards' and Kaul's mark. It would appear, therefore, that the business of Edwards and Kaul lacked a master silversmith and except for special exhibition pieces what was previously a manufacturing business developed into an importing jewellery and English silver retailing shop.

The evidence as to Edwards' business at 31 and 85 Collins Street, being a manufacturing one, may be deduced by the number of items bearing other retailers marks, such as Walsh Bros, Joseph & Co., Pall Mall, Sandhurst and Kilpatrick & Co.

They utilised indigenous products such as the emu and swan eggs, the burra nut, opal and pearl for home presents, making these into varied forms of gold and silver plate and jewellery. They obtained high praise, supplying gifts for the Duke of Edinburgh in 1867, the Garibaldi sword (lost) and a gold casket presented to a Captain Standish (lost), which was a masterpiece of art, in addition to numerous gold cups, trowels, dinner services etc. It is fitting then that Edwards was honoured by the Royal visitor of 1867, and appointed goldsmith and jeweller to the Royal Household because of the fine work he produced for the Duke of Edinburgh.

F.N.H.

135 A fine large and heavy early presentation cup and cover. With applied cast silver band of vine leaves, fruit and tendrils, cast silver handles leading to a fluted bowl, the stem supported on an octofoil base embossed with kangaroos and emus. The finial to the lid is missing. The lid has an embossed floral decorated top, the border is cast and applied.
Inscription: "Melbourne Hunt Club Cup won by Bobby ridden by his owner, James Bevan, Esq., October 8, 1859".

MAKER: W. Edwards, Melbourne. WEIGHT: 80 ozs. HEIGHT: 35 cm.
CIRCA: 1859 Private Collection, Victoria.

136 A fine presentation tray and claret jug en suite. The claret jug of elegant shape decorated with applied vine leaves, the tray with cast applied feet in the form of grape vine leaves and tendrils, applied cast grape vine border and well engraved floral centre depicting flowers, grapes and fruits to a cartouche.
Inscription: "Presented to John Armstrong Riack, Esq., of the Oriental Bank Corporation as a token of esteem by his friends at Pleasant Creek on his leaving the Colony of Victoria, July 31st, 1864".

MAKER: W. Edwards, Melbourne and retailed by Walsh & Sons, Melbourne.
CLARET JUG: Weight: 31 ozs. Height: 32 cm.
TRAY: Weight: 32 ozs. Width: 33 cm.
CIRCA: 1863 Private Collection, Victoria.
ILLUSTRATED

137 A fine claret jug with applied curved wreath of vine leaves to the plain pear shaped body standing on an octofoil base, engraved "Geelong & Western Districts Hunt Club Steeplechase, September 26th 1863 etc."

MAKER: W. Edwards, Melbourne. WEIGHT: 24 ozs. HEIGHT: 36 cm.
CIRCA: 1863 Tamworth City Council, Regan Collection.

Item 136 (part)

138 A fine Australian claret jug with cast handle, grape and vine leaf decoration. Set in the body four cast applied plaques of a kingfisher, an aboriginal with boomerang and shield, a lyrebird and a scene of two aboriginals. The emu finial is missing but the whole item bears many similarities to Edwards' work. See lid of 1867 Queen's Plate for similar raised plaques.

MAKER: Attributed to W. Edwards, Melbourne, but unmarked.
WEIGHT: 23 ozs. HEIGHT: 33 cm. CIRCA: 1865 COLLECTION: The Reserve Bank

139 A fine claret jug, the elongated, tapered pear shaped body applied with embossed vine leaves and grape decoration.
Inscription: "Presented as a token of respect to Brother Hewison, P.M. by the Adelaide Lodge, August 1866".

MAKER: William Edwards, Melbourne. WEIGHT: 32 ozs. HEIGHT: 33 cm.
CIRCA: 1865 COLLECTION: Museum of Applied Arts and Sciences, Sydney.

140 A fine globular shape claret jug. Raised on an octofoil embossed grape vine base, the globular shape made in two sections, the top clamping on to the base for cleaning, with pierced and finely chased vine leaves and bunches of grapes, the lid surmounted by a finial depicting grape leaves and grapes with grape vine handle. Complete with original velvet lined cedar travelling box.

MAKER: William Edwards, Melbourne. WEIGHT: 27 ozs. HEIGHT: 33 cm.
CIRCA: 1865 COLLECTION: J. Patience, Esq., Sydney.

141 A good goblet, the bowl embossed with plain oval medallions set amongst water lillies and bullrushes.

MAKER: W. Edwards, Melbourne. WEIGHT: 10 ozs. HEIGHT: 19 cm.
CIRCA: 1865 COLLECTION: D. Paul, Esq., Sydney.

142 A good cricketing trophy in the form of a bell shaped cup with a wreathed bat and stump on circular foot chased in high relief. One side embossed with an elaborate scene of a cricket match in progress, to other inscribed: "Presented to W. Moore Bell, Esq., by the Winners."

MAKER: W. Edwards, Melbourne. WEIGHT: 23 ozs. HEIGHT: 29.5 cm.
CIRCA: 1865 COLLECTION: F. McDonald, Esq., Sydney.

143 A fine and rare cast silver candle stick of a cherub holding up a stylised grape-vine with hanging bunches of grapes and grape leaves to the stem.

MAKER: W. Edwards, Melbourne. WEIGHT: 27 ozs. HEIGHT: 36 cm.
WIDTH: 16 cm. CIRCA: 1865 COLLECTION: Mr & Mrs J. Hopkins, Victoria.

144 A good silver goblet with applied cast decoration to the inscription cartouches, the balance of the body florally embossed, the base embossed with emus and kangaroos on a standard Edwards octofoil plinth.

MAKER: W. Edwards, Melbourne. WEIGHT: 11 ozs. HEIGHT: 25 cm.
CIRCA: 1865 Private Collection, Adelaide.

145 An extremely fine and rare large soup tureen and cover with applied gadrooned border to the lid surmounted by a good cast finial. The plain oval body with applied cartouches inscriptions erased and cast handles. The embossed gadroon oval base matching the decoration in the lid.

MAKER: W. Edwards, Melbourne. WEIGHT: 88 ozs. HEIGHT: 35 cm.
WIDTH: 38 cm. CIRCA: 1865 Tamworth City Council, Regan Collection.
ILLUSTRATED

146 A fine and rare lidded tankard of 18th century form. The plain body with embossed acanthus leaf decoration matched in the lid with applied cast handle and finial.

MAKER: W. Edwards, Melbourne. WEIGHT: 30 ozs. HEIGHT: 21½ cms.
CIRCA: 1865 Tamworth City Council, Regan Collection.

147 A good novel inkwell constructed from half an emu egg, the ink pots decorated with Greek key pattern borders, the oval plinth surmounting the half emu egg terminating in ringed lion's head handles on palm tree octofoil base.

MAKER: William Edwards, Melbourne. OVERALL WEIGHT: 20 ozs.
HEIGHT: 20 cm. CIRCA: 1865 COLLECTION: K. Fahy, Esq., Sydney.

NB: The Greek key pattern borders are peculiar to the work of two Melbourne makers, Edwards and Fischer.

148 A fine and rare large meat cover, the whole raised from the flat, marked in the top of the lid. Gadroon border to the edge.

MAKER: W. Edwards, Melbourne. WEIGHT: 70 ozs. HEIGHT: 30 cm.
WIDTH: 44 cm. CIRCA: 1865 Private Collection, Victoria.
ILLUSTRATED

149 A good plain goblet, raised from the flat.
Inscription: "Presented by the Members of the Clunes Accident Relief Fund to J. H. Richmond, Esq., 1865."

MAKER: W. Edwards, Melbourne, retailed by Kilpatrick & Co. WEIGHT: 11 ozs.
HEIGHT: 23 cm. CIRCA: 1865 COLLECTION: Mr & Mrs J. D. Altmann,
Melbourne.

Item 145

Item 148

150 An extremely fine and rare racing trophy surmounted by a cast figure of a race horse, the lid with six inset silver gilt plaques of racing scenes each with finely pierced decorative border. The bowl inset with four well cast horses heads, the simulated reins of linked chain joined to three cast cherubs on the stem. The base with complete embossed racing scene bears the inscription: "Queens Plate won by Tim Whiffler 1867".

> *MAKER: William Edwards, Melbourne. WEIGHT: 112 ozs.*
> *OVERALL HEIGHT including plinth: 74 cm. CIRCA: 1866*
> *COLLECTION: J. Royds, Esq.*
> *ILLUSTRATED IN COLOUR ON DUST JACKET*

151 A fine and interesting presentation casket, supported on two fern trees supporting a silver mounted emu egg with silver gilt interior, surmounted by a group of emus as a finial. Almost identical to that illustrated in The Illustrated Melbourne Post, 10-9-1868, made by Joseph & Co., as retailers but on the evidence of this item manufactured by W. Edwards.

> *MAKER: W. Edwards, Melbourne. WEIGHT: 38 ozs. HEIGHT: 33 cm.*
> *LENGTH: 23 cm. CIRCA: 1868 COLLECTION: B. Caillard, Esq., Victoria.*

152 A good embossed goblet with no inscription, marked with Royal Appointment mark.

MAKER: W. Edwards, Melbourne. WEIGHT: 8 ozs. HEIGHT: 19 cm. WIDTH: 8 cm. CIRCA: 1870 Private Collection, Victoria.

153 A good and unusual inkwell on cedar plinth, in the form of a fitted mounted emu egg with silver gilt interior. The oval Greek key pattern base decorated with cast emu and kangaroo from which issues a fern trunk holding the egg with four fern leaves. Lion mask ringed side handles. With Royal Appointment mark.

MAKER: W. Edwards, Melbourne. OVERALL WEIGHT: 36 ozs. HEIGHT: 26 cm. CIRCA: 1870 Tamworth City Council, Regan Collection.

154 A mounted emu egg goblet silver gilt lined on entwined vine stem to the embossed octofoil base.

MAKER: W. Edwards, Melbourne. OVERALL WEIGHT: 8 ozs. HEIGHT: 19 cm. WIDTH: 9 cm. CIRCA: 1870 Private Collection, Victoria.

155 A mounted emu egg goblet with silver gilt interior on palm tree stem to octofoil base covered with embossed floral decoration.

MAKER: William Edwards, Melbourne. OVERALL WEIGHT: 8 ozs. HEIGHT: 16 cm. CIRCA: 1870 COLLECTION: F. McDonald, Esq., Sydney.

156 A mounted emu egg goblet with silver gilt interior on palm tree stem to octofoil base covered with embossed floral decoration.

MAKER: William Edwards, Melbourne. OVERALL WEIGHT: 9 ozs. HEIGHT: 21 cm. CIRCA: 1870 COLLECTION: F. McDonald, Esq., Sydney.

157 A good heavy presentation goblet with embossed decoration, raised from the flat, prick marked in the top, Edwards Melbourne.
Inscription: "National Agricultural Society President's Cup for the Best Shorthorn Bull 1873".

MAKER: W. Edwards, Melbourne. WEIGHT: 11 ozs. HEIGHT: 20 cm. MAXIMUM WIDTH: 10 cm. CIRCA: 1870 Private Collection, Melbourne.

158 A fine scent bottle holder on beaded octofoil base, embossed with scenes of emus and kangaroos, leading to a divided emu egg, leather covered to the exterior, silver gilt liners to the interior, with decorated handles of flowers. The inside containing two cut glass, silver mounted scent bottles. The finial, depicting a parakeet amongst grape vines, tendrils and fruit, presses down to open and shut the egg. Marked in the base of the holder. The perfume bottles which are presumably English, are unmarked.

> *MAKER: W. Edwards, Melbourne. WEIGHT: 26 ozs. HEIGHT: 32 cm.*
> *MAXIMUM OPEN WIDTH: 29 cm. CIRCA: 1870 Private Collection, Victoria.*

NB: Steiner possibly copies this idea from Edwards.

159 A good silver mounted emu egg ink well by Edwards, with silver gilt handles surmounted by an emu in foliage. The group pivots to disclose a removable ink well which is signed on the base.

> *MAKER: W. Edwards, Melbourne. WEIGHT: 13 ozs. HEIGHT: 22 cm. WIDTH: 15 cm.*
> *CIRCA: 1870 COLLECTION: B. Caillard, Esq., Victoria.*

160 A good embossed goblet with no inscription, marked with Royal Appointment mark, on octafoil beaded base.

> *MAKER: W. Edwards, Melbourne. WEIGHT: 8 ozs. HEIGHT: 19 cm. WIDTH: 8 cm.*
> *CIRCA: 1870 Private Collection, Victoria.*

161 A plain, well made goblet in two sections, the bowl screwing into the stem at a concealed junction at the base.

> *MAKER: W, Edwards, Melbourne. WEIGHT: 6 ozs. HEIGHT: 18 cm.*
> *CIRCA: 1870 COLLECTION: B. Caillard, Esq., Victoria.*

ALFRED WALSH (1837-1917)
WALSH & SONS (Alfred and Frederick)
WALSH BROS. (Alfred and Frederick)

WALSH, Alfred Snr., started the firm approximately 1850 in a shop between Flinders Street and Flinders Lane. By 1859 he had taken his eldest son, Alfred, into the business and moved to 53 Collins Street East, where he advertised as a watchmaker, silversmith and jeweller. By 1864 as evidenced by the claret jug by Edwards, retailed by Walsh & Sons, his other brother, Frederick, had been taken into the business, The firm became Walsh Bros. on the retirement of the father, Circa 1865, exhibiting the Melbourne Exhibition 1866-1867 as Walsh Bros., 53 Collins Street, Melbourne. They exhibited, besides other articles of value, two massive silver cups, the one for the Gippsland Meeting (lost) and the other offered by Messrs. J. Levy & Sons, as a prize for the best growth of Silesian beet. (lost)

Walsh Bros. were essentially retailers and not manufacturers, their main supplier would have been William Edwards, numerous articles survive to prove this with their joint marks. Moss and Caspar also made articles for them. The partnership became one of the largest jewellery businesses in the state of Victoria, being sold up in 1881.   **F.N.H.**

162 A fine and rare set of eight finger bowls. I think it is a fair assumption to say that they are possibly by W. Edwards, as Walsh retailed most of Edwards' work at this date.
Inscription: "To Hugh George for upholding the liberty rights of the Press, Melbourne 1866".

RETAILERS: Walsh Bros., Melbourne. TOTAL WEIGHT: 36 ozs., approx. 4 ozs. each. HEIGHT: 3 cm. DIAMETER: 11 cm.
CIRCA: 1865 Private Collection, Victoria.
ILLUSTRATED

Item 162

163 A good goblet with three lily flowers, three bullrushes, three leaves emerging from the tapering stem to hold the bowl which is inscribed "Melbourne Regatta Upper Yarra, 1868, Grand Challenge Cup".

MAKER: Walsh Bros., Melbourne. WEIGHT: 7 ozs. HEIGHT: 25 cm.
CIRCA: 1868 Tamworth City Council, Regan Collection.

164 Presentation goblet inscribed with Royal Coat of Arms in a circle, on the band of the circle, St. Kilda and a mermaid floating in the sea,
Inscription: "St. Kilda Amateur Sailing Match won by . . . from a few friends".

MAKER: Moss and Caspar. RETAILERS: Walsh Bros.
WEIGHT: 7 ozs. HEIGHT: 24 cm. MAXIMUM WIDTH: 10 cm.
CIRCA: 1870 Private Collection, Melbourne.

165 A fine large silver racing trophy on stand, punch marked Walsh Bros. It has certain stylistic affinities with Fischer of Geelong's work, An embossed racing scene to one side, to the reverse a cartouche with the inscription: "Southern Hunt Club Cup won by Mr G. J. C. Lords' True Blue, ridden by George Law, 1876".

WEIGHT: 23 ozs. HEIGHT: 26 cm. MAX OVERALL WIDTH: excluding stand: 25 cm. CIRCA: 1875 Private Collection, Adelaide.

JOHN HAMMERTON & SON

HAMMERTON, John & Son, Little Ryrie Street, Geelong, established in 1879 were "working jewellers, diamond setters, engravers and designers, with watches and jewellery etc. in stock."
They designed and executed in 15 carat gold, an 8 oz presentation piece for his Royal Highness the Prince of Wales in 1919. The present was a letter weight containing a representation of an Australian shield decorated with native flora and fauna.
In 1927 they fashioned in 15 carat for the Duke of York a correspondence clip with the Geelong City Crest, and an embossed wreath of laurel combined with shamrock and thistle, held by a rose; the Duchess received an old boomerang with tribal markings, mounted in gold and with the city crest. Each was enclosed in a fiddle-back case of blackwood.
On 14th September, 1927, J. Hammerton died, and an obituary advised that he was famed throughout the country for handsome specimens of the goldsmiths' craft, gold and silver cups, racing trophies, mayoral chains etc. His hobby was collecting rarities of the South Sea Islands which he presented to the City of Geelong. His brother was a retail jeweller in Mildura.

F.N.B.

166 Thin lightweight trophy, presumably made on a budget.

MAKER: J. Hammerton, Geelong. WEIGHT: 9 ozs. HEIGHT: 26 cm. WIDTH: 15 cm.
CIRCA: 1891 COLLECTION: Mr & Mrs J. D. Altmann, Melbourne.

DENIS BROS.

DENIS Bros., watchmakers, manufacturing jewellers, opticians and importers, 257-261 Bourke Street, Melbourne, were founded by Mr Sylla Denis who arrived from France in 1853. After a short time at the gold fields in Ballarat he returned to Melbourne and started business as a watch and clock repairer.

Victor, his brother, joined him in 1866; then Gustave Lachal was admitted as a partner. Lachal retired from the business in 1888, and both Sylla and Victor died in 1889 within a few months of each other. Ferdinand, only son of Sylla, carried on the business. "A speciality, stock of ecclesiastical wares used in celebrating Roman Catholic Divine services, together with beautiful vestments, made a very rich and artistic display", is a quote from a newspaper of the time.

Obtained first order of merit award for gold and silver jewellery at the Melbourne International Exhibition, 1880-1881.   **F.N.H.**

167 Pair of silver mounted emu egg jugs with well engraved decoration standing on ebonised plinths.

   Maker: Denis Bros., Melbourne. OVERALL WEIGHT: 15 ozs. HEIGHT: 31 cm. CIRCA: 1870 COLLECTION: Mr & Mrs J. D. Altmann, Melbourne.

168 An extremely fine and rare chalice with cast applied decoration and pierced lobed base.

   MAKER: Denis Bros., Melbourne. WEIGHT: 24 oz. HEIGHT: 23 cm. CIRCA: 1870 Private Collection, Sydney.
                    ILLUSTRATED

GEORGE H. ARMFIELD

ARMFIELD, George H., Stanley Street, Collingwood, Victoria, was born in Croydon, England, and came to the colonies when very young, arriving in Melbourne from South Australia in 1867. He learned the watch and jewellery making craft with Messrs Wenzel & Enes, Bourke Street, in whose employ he remained until 1878, when he established his own business at Stanley Street, Collingwood. As business prospered he enlarged the premises from time to time. By 1888 he employed ten men and four boys.

His trade was divided into the two distinct compartments, that of watch and clock making and repairing, and jewellery manufacturing. The latter contained a large machine for cutting discs and medals, wire and plate rolling machines, and a large machine for stamping medals. A specialty was medal making, masonic and friendly society emblems etc.

Mr. Armfield received a certificate at the Melbourne Exhibition of 1880 for jewellery exhibits and was the donor of the "Armfield Bucket Trophy" presented annually for junior cricket competition in the eighteen eighties. (lost)   **F.N.H.**

Item 168

169 A fine and unusual christening present depicting a cradle towed by a swan over which hangs a suspended cherub holding the reins. The cradle is silver gilt and the swan to the front is cast and well finished. In the base support is a medal, "City of Collingwood, 1855" and it bears the Collingwood Coat of Arms.

    MAKER: George H. Armfield, Collingwood.
    WEIGHT: 34 ozs. WIDTH: 22 cm. HEIGHT: 17 cm.
    CIRCA: 1870 COLLECTION: Mr & Mrs J. D. Altmann, Melbourne.
                       ILLUSTRATED

Item 169

EDWARD FRANCIS GUNTER FISCHER

FISCHER, Edward Francis Gunter, of Kirk Place, Geelong (1828-?), jeweller, goldsmith and watchmaker, born in Vienna. He arrived in Victoria in the mid 1850's, and married Sarah Potswin, born Cheltenham, England, at Geelong in 1859.

One of Australia's finest goldsmiths. There is a record of Edward R. Fischer in Geelong and District Directories from 1858, but he may have arrived earlier. Advertising variously under the heading for jewellers and watchmakers he was initially at Kirk Place, and from 1882 at Ryrie Street, and the business moved to Melbourne about 1895.

In its 1882-1883 issue the Newtown and Chilwell Directory included this advertisement: "Edward Fischer, Practical Jeweller and Watchmaker, Great Ryrie Street East, Geelong. Splendid Stock of Gold and Silver Goods, Electroplated Ware, Clocks and Watches at Most Reasonable Prices. All orders executed on the premises, workshops may be inspected."

Fischer moved from Geelong to Collins Street, Melbourne, as city directories from 1895 to 1916 list a firm of watchmakers at 190 Collins Street, the name appearing as "E. Fischer & Son" or as "Edward Fischer & Son. (Fischer, Edward and Harry C.) Many years in Geelong. Jewellers, 190 Collins Street. Private address 23 Wattletree Road, Armadale."

In 1904 there is a similar entry but Edward no longer appears as a partner. Harry C. Fischer seems to have continued operating the business until about 1916.

Fischer's trophy plate would possibly be among the best known 19th century work in Victoria if not Australia. The long period (1858-1916) in which gold and silver might bear his surname may mean that far more collectors have a representative piece than hitherto suspected. However, it is known that Americans have taken his work back to their country. Not all of his work is stamped with his name and district.

Known remaining works include: Globular teapot; emu egg mounted in silver as vase; Ciborium 1870, Trophy Cup, with finial of Pegasus, 1875 (unmarked); silver trophy cup, Geelong College, 1882, for mile walking race; silver trophy cup 1884; silver trophy cup 1886.

Though Fischer did not generally exhibit his plate or jewellery at the large 19th Century Exhibitions, he provided Exhibit No. 290 Gold and Silver Cups, Racing Trophies, etc., at the International Exhibition, Melbourne 1880-1881. As a stylist he was first class, placing emphasis on beauty of design and shape and finishing work with excellent chasing. Though, perhaps, his work was not so rich in repousse as was that of Edwards, he invariably succeeded in producing plate and jewellery which is a delight to use, handle, wear or observe.

To Fischer may go the honour of being the first designer and manufacturer of the first locally produced Melbourne Cup in 1865.   **F.N.H.**

170 A very fine and rare 18 ct. gold racing trophy with applied gold lettering, "Geelong Races 1880" engraved square handles, fitted with a detachable stopper surmounted by a finial of a race horse mounted at the gallop. The base of the race horse decorated with a Greek key patterned border.

MAKER: Fischer of Geelong, (lid only marked). Base stamped 18 ct. gold.
WEIGHT: 21 ozs. HEIGHT: 34 cm. WIDTH: 16½ cm.
CIRCA: 1880 Private Collection, Victoria.
ILLUSTRATED

Item 170

171 A fine heavy claret jug with square engraved handle and floral decoration to the body, a Greek key pattern border to the foot and top of the body. Almost en suite with this in style is a small goblet again raised from the flat, marked Sterling Silver, with the same punches as those used on the claret jug, and decorated with the same Greek key pattern border to the base and top of the bowl.
Inscription on claret jug: "Presented to Dr. Wilkie by the members of the Great Waradgery OAF, in appreciation of his services as a great surgeon and as a mark of esteem, February 23, 1882."

MAKER: E. Fischer, Geelong. WEIGHT: 22 ozs. HEIGHT: 32 cm. WIDTH: 13 cm.
CIRCA: 1882 Private Collection, Melbourne.
ILLUSTRATED

172 A similar goblet inscribed Melbourne Regatta 1876 Maiden Year won by W. Snedden, Footscray Rowing Club."

MAKER: Attributed to Fischer, Geelong. WEIGHT: 4 ozs. HEIGHT: 16 cm.
CIRCA: 1875 Private Collection, Melbourne.

173 A well engraved goblet with a representation of Hibernia weeping to one side and an early Australian coat of arms to the other.

MAKER: E. Fischer, Geelong. WEIGHT: 5 ozs. HEIGHT: 16½ cm.
CIRCA: 1880 COLLECTION: B. Caillard, Esq., Victoria.

174 A good chess trophy, the finial surmounting the trophy is in the form of a knight, engraved to the body of the trophy two gentlemen playing chess, the handles entwined allegorical snakes. The whole raised from the flat.

MAKER: E. Fischer, Geelong. WEIGHT: 18 ozs. HEIGHT: 25 cm. MAX WIDTH: 15 cm.
CIRCA: 1880 Private Collection, Melbourne.

175 A small silver pap boat with crimped edge.

MAKER: E. Fischer, Geelong. WEIGHT: 3 ozs. HEIGHT: 11 cm.
CIRCA: 1880 Private Collection, Victoria.

Item 171

H. YOUNG & COMPANY

No early history of the Youngs can presently be put forward—but in 1880, Thomas Young was living in Kew; and in partnership with his son Henry H. Young, in Little Collins Street, west, Melbourne; they traded as T. Young & Son, "manufacturing gold and silversmiths." In 1884 Henry Young & Co., had premises at 49/51 Collins Street, east, while Thomas, his father, continued as "Thomas Young & Son" at his old address. It is suggested that silverwares were still made at the father's workshop, and sold through the son's business. In this way, such wares could carry the son's name, as seller.

176 Lipped jug, marked H. Young & Co. Of good gauge, well engraved with fern leaves to front and sides and in oval panel on one side opposite the inscription is a gentleman firing a gun in a paddock.
Inscription: "Melbourne Gun Club Trophy presented by Members of the Club won by W. D. Clark, 14th July, 1883".

MAKER: H. Young, Melbourne. WEIGHT: 14 ozs. HEIGHT: 13 cm.
MAX WIDTH: 18 cm. CIRCA: 1880 Private Collection, Melbourne.

JAMES McBEAN & SON

McBEAN, James & Son (William), watchmakers and jewellers, etc., "The Block" Elizabeth Street, were established in 1858 by Mr J. McBean. The second generation Mr McBean was actively engaged in business from 1850 until 1890. Though he took no active part in public matters his name was well known.

The founder, James, was born in Inverness, Scotland, in 1833, serving apprenticeship as a jeweller and watchmaker there. On arriving in Australia he saw immense possibilities.

Once established, the business increased. In 1894 operations were carried on in a well appointed place; a most noticeable feature being the lavish display of work in gold and silver.

A large quantity of the jewellery was manufactured by the firm, and compared very favourably with that turned out in England. In 1890 Mr McBean senior retired and handed over to William, now with 20 years experience. William was born in Melbourne in 1858, and was interested in the Melbourne Cricket Club. A member of the committee, he was one of the Committee of Management looking after the English team of 1901. He died in 1921.   **F.N.H.**

177 An unusual ornamental inkstand in the form of a silver mounted emu egg, surmounted by a kangaroo and drawn along on a bizarre carriage decorated with vines attached to an emu with an aboriginal on its back, the pen rest with bird finials.

MAKER: James McBean & Son, Melbourne. HEIGHT: 27 cm. LENGTH: 32 cm.
CIRCA: 1870 COLLECTION: B. Boulken Pty. Ltd., Sydney.

KILPATRICK & CO.

KILPATRICK & CO., gold and silversmiths, jewellers and watchmakers, were established in Melbourne in 1853 as a wholesale house at 20 Queen Street, where trade was carried on for two years. In 1855, a second business was opened at 39 Collins Street West, removed later to 12 Collins Street.

The Age 7-1-1861: "Kilpatrick & Co., 39 Collins Street West, continue to receive every month, by overland mail, supplies of presentation and family plate, an inspection of which is invited. Articles of colonial manufacture tastefully got up and estimates furnished. Illustrated catalogue may be had gratis on application."

For the 1866 Exhibition in Melbourne, the work of Kilpatrick & Co., silversmiths, received the following report: "Messrs Kilpatrick & Co. exhibited sets of jewellery rich with brilliants as well as a large silver cup intended for a racing prize."

By 1858, John Thompson, partner in the original firm, was sole proprietor of the business which gave, by then, an average employment to 20 workers, including apprentices, doing extensive manufacturing themselves as well as letting out a large amount of work to outside artisans. Drummonds eventually took over the business.

Kilpatrick & Co. were responsible for the local production of the mace in the Victorian Legislative Assembly in 1901 and James Holt is the accredited craftsman of the piece. The mace is described as follows: "The new mace has been manufactured by Messrs Kilpatrick & Co. of Collins Street, and is made of silver, gilded over so that it presents the appearance of solid gold. The silver, over 250 oz of which were used in its construction, is wrought into a variety of beautiful designs. The bulb on which rests the crown is decorated with four badges in repousse work, representing the rose, harp, thistle and Victorian Waratah. On the top of the stave, which is nearly five feet long, are the Australian arms, motto and garter in fine chased work, and the whole is surmounted by the orb and cross. The stem of the mace is ornamented with roses, thistles and shamrocks, twined about with a ribbon, on which are engraved the names of all the Speakers who have occupied the chair in the Victorian Legislative Assembly since responsible government was inaugurated."   **F.N.H.**

178 Small goblet, well engraved with individual flora and fauna, butterflies, parakeets, and marked with the retailers mark, Kilpatrick & Company.
Inscription: "St. Kilda Yacht Race, 1884-5 Trophy presented by Mr J. McQuie, Jnr. won by Mr Myers' Camilla".

RETAILERS: Kilpatrick & Co. WEIGHT: 4 ozs. HEIGHT: 18 cm.
CIRCA: 1885 Private Collection, Melbourne.
ILLUSTRATED

Item 178

179 Kangaroo paper weights.

MAKER: Kilpatrick & Co., Melbourne. WEIGHT: 11 and 12 ozs. HEIGHT: 18 and 21 cm. CIRCA: 1900 COLLECTION: J. B. Hawkins, Antiques.
ILLUSTRATED

Item 179

DRUMMONDS OF MELBOURNE

DRUMMOND, William (1838-1917) was born in Stirling, Scotland, and arrived in Melbourne on the ship "Marco Polo" in 1860, at once establishing himself as a jeweller in Collins Street, In 1872 he joined Mr Brush (q.v.) and the firm of Brush & Drummond became well known. His partner pre-deceased him and the business came under his own name as sole proprietor.

Drummond personally conducted the business to the very last until his sight failed as he was extremely interested in all the aspects of his fine manufacturing and retail establishment as well as the commissioning work by our best goldsmiths.

Before his death he had taken the opportunity to donate £1,000 to the Royal Institute for the Blind and gave a number of oil paintings to the National Gallery of Victoria in 1913.

Twice married, he was a widower at his death and left no family. As the business was still a private one he bequeathed it to his nephew Andrew Drummond.

DRUMMOND, Andrew (1880-1957) nephew of the founder, William, came to Australia in 1899 and at William's death in 1917 took over the business as sole proprietor. He was well known as a sportsman, also as one of the leaders of the jewellery trade in Australia. During times when their fashionable and exclusive jewellery was at peak demand, Drummonds had up to 26 artisans in their own workshop.

With hard times in the 1890's and afterwards, this number fell to a very few craftsmen. The interest in gold and silver has tended to be capricious for the worker in those metals, and the very exclusive lines were affected.

In 1950 the business was converted to a public company and late in the sixties a change of establishment was made to just around the corner from Collins Street, where they had become the Mecca of Victorian Jewellery for about a century, to Bourke Street.

Drummonds have a watch register which dates back to 1857 and includes the names of many pioneer families.

The 1891 Melbourne Cup won by Malvolio was made by the firm and is possibly the grandest of all the Melbourne Cup trophies. Upon a base of chased silver the figure of Victory stands on a dais and holds out an olive wreath to the mounted jockey. The figures in silver are superbly modelled. The whole piece, about two feet long by 15 inches high rested on a stand of ebony. See illustration "The First Tuesday in November" by D. L. Bernstein, page 225. (lost)

British smiths won the commission for some years, but in 1915 the Victoria Racing Club ordered on Drummonds again.   **F.N.H.**

180 A fine large heavy standing emu paper weight, mounted on oval matted plinth.

> *MAKER: Drummond, Melbourne, marked pure Australian silver.*
> *WEIGHT: 26 ozs. HEIGHT: 13 cm. CIRCA: 1900*
> *COLLECTION: J. B. Hawkins Antiques.*
> *ILLUSTRATED*

Item 180

THOMAS STOKES
STOKES (AUSTRALASIA) LTD.

STOKES, Thomas arrived in Melbourne about 1854. He was a die sinker and button maker in 1856, at 115 Flinders Street East. Among 19th century Australian medallists he is credited with having issued more tokens, if not more varieties, than any other token maker, and for having produced the first tokens of truly Australian design and motif.

In 1870 he took Mr Martin into partnership. On undated penny tokens they advertised their trade as Die Sinkers, Seal Engravers, Medallists, Button, Check, Token, Military and Masonic Ornament Makers, 100 Collins Street East, Melbourne.

In 1873 Thomas made a major addition to his work by introducing silverware. At this time his factory was 100 Collins Street. His four sons learned the secrets of his craft. Harry was first to join in the business, later to be followed by Fred, Tom and Vincent.

In 1895 the firm became Stokes & Son, and two years later Stokes & Sons.

In 1875 Thomas made a handsome ewer modelled as a replica of a mounted emu egg. In 1880 he fashioned an epergne out of local silver which was a special display piece at the International Exhibition held at the Exhibition Building, Carlton, Melbourne, in that year.

On 17th September, 1907, Stokes & Sons applied for registration of Australian trade mark comprising the figure of a kangaroo preceding the old court letter S in a six pointed star, and the word KANGAROO underneath, for their precious metals work.

Another trade mark was registered for precious metals on 7th December, 1920. Again the ornate S was in a six pointed star above a boomerang.   **F.N.H.**

UNASCRIBED OR UNMARKED PIECES
POSSIBLY BY VICTORIAN SILVERSMITHS

181 Inkwell mounted in half an emu egg with Greek key pattern handles, the finial of the inkwell a kangaroo, embossed foliage, the border to the base of the inkwell exactly the same as the previous item.

Unmarked, possibly Edwards, Melbourne.
WEIGHT: 12 ozs. HEIGHT: 26½ cm. WIDTH: 11 cm.
CIRCA: 1870 COLLECTION: Mr & Mrs J. D. Altmann, Melbourne.

182 A fine unmarked claret jug with beaded borders. It is interesting to note the method of applying the grape vine decoration to the body is as that used by Edwards with moveable screws in the form of vine leaves for attaching it to the body.
Inscription: "Presented to H. Rickson, Esq., as a mark of esteem from his friends on his completing the growing line of railway and leaving the Ballarat district, November 1st, 1879."

MAKER: Unknown, possibly very late Edwards work.
WEIGHT: 20 ozs. HEIGHT: 32 cm. MAX WIDTH: including handle: 15 cm.
CIRCA: 1879 Private Collection, Melbourne.

183 Emu egg silver mounted cup mounted on a cedar plinth and decorated with fern leaves to the base of the bowl. With unusual Greek key pattern straight handles terminating in aboriginal head masks. Presentation inscription for 1873: "Presented to C. Clark, Esq., by the Students of the School of Design, Public Library Melbourne, 1873."

MAKER: Unsigned, possibly Edwards, Melbourne. OVERALL WEIGHT: 30 ozs. HEIGHT: 49 cm. CIRCA: 1873 COLLECTION: Mr & Mrs J. D. Altmann, Melbourne.

184 Set of four decanter labels, whisky, sherry, rum and brandy. Well engraved and marked to the back Sterling Silver, a large kangaroo and makers mark, WK. It may be South Australia.

WEIGHT: 2 ozs. DIMENSIONS: 4 cm x 2 cm. CIRCA: 1900 Private collection, Victoria.

185 A fine and rare carved silver gilt mounted emu egg, surmounted by an emu. Carved on one side with a pair of kangaroos, on the other side with a koala bear and a possum. Marked CB and M and a queen in one mark, and CB, a lion and a leopards head in another mark.

WEIGHT: 9 ozs. OVERALL HEIGHT: 25 cm. CARVING SIGNED: J. Heath. CIRCA: 1860 COLLECTION: Mr & Mrs J. D. Altmann, Melbourne.

186 A fine and heavy mounted emu egg, silver gilt lined, the finial comprising a pair of cockatoos over a nestful of eggs, the handles a pair of possums, to palm fronds emerging from the trunk of a palm tree down which a goanna is climbing. The embossed base mounted with a pair of aboriginal figures of a male and female, the female carrying a gourd and a baby on its back in blackened silver. Of extremely fine quality and weight, inscribed and dated 1869.

MAKER: Unknown. WEIGHT: 26 ozs. HEIGHT: 30 cm. WIDTH: 24 cm. CIRCA: 1869 COLLECTION: Mr & Mrs J. D. Altmann, Melbourne.

187 A good goblet with embossed, raised decoration on octofoil base bearing many similarities to the work of William Edwards. A raised decorative picture of a gold or silver mine to one side to the reverse a plain shield bounded by two embossed trees.

MAKER: Unknown. MARKS: LTS an emu and kangaroo. WEIGHT: 12 oz. HEIGHT: 20 cm. CIRCA: 1870 Tamworth City Council, Regan Collection.

188 An inkwell, the two handles comprising bunches of grapes and leaves. The finial of the inkwell, an emu standing amongst foliage.

MAKER: Unmarked, possibly by Edwards, Melbourne. WEIGHT: 6 ozs. HEIGHT: 18 cm. WIDTH: 16 cm. CIRCA: 1870 COLLECTION: Mr & Mrs J. D. Altmann, Melbourne.

DAVID BARCLAY

BARCLAY, David is believed to have been Tasmania's first silversmith. From information provided by the State Library of Tasmania and his grand-daughter it is known that he was born at Montrose, Scotland, about 1804 and arrived at Hobart Town from London by the "Resource" in October 1830. In 1831 he advertised in The Hobart Town Courier as a watch and clock maker and that he had removed to premises in Elizabeth Street. In June 1832 he married Margaret Strachan at St. David's Church Hobart. They had five sons and two daughters. He died at Hobart 22nd August, 1884.

A James Barclay, possibly his brother, arrived in Tasmania during 1834 and established himself as a watchmaker and jeweller at Launceston. Recorded items by D. Barclay include a silver salver presented in 1838 to Captain Alexander Mackenzie for his efforts in the capture of bushrangers (illustrated in The Australasian Antique Collector No. 2 1967)—whereabouts unknown, a silver salver presented in 1841 to the Rev. James Garrett by Miss Horne on behalf of the Bothwell Literary Society and 55 other inhabitants in the district (coll. Tasmanian Museum and Art Gallery, Hobart) and a silver cup presented to George Augustus Robinson in 1835 by the inhabitants of Bothwell (coll. Queen Victoria Museum and Art Gallery, Launceston).

K.F.

189 A very fine and rare heavy pair of silver salvers with elaborate repousse decoration depicting flora and fauna including the emu and kangaroo. The salvers are inscribed—"Presented by Members of the legal Profession in Van Diemen's Land to Alfred Stephen Esq. (formerly Attorney General of that Colony) upon his promotion to the Bench of New South Wales 16th April, 1839".

(*See The Australasian Antique Collector, No. 14, 1973*)

*MAKER: D. Barclay, Tasmania. DIAMETER: 30 cm. WEIGHT: 30 oz. each
CIRCA: 1839 Private Collection, Sydney.*
ILLUSTRATED

Alfred Stephen (1802-1894) was born at St. Kitts in the West Indies. In 1824, the year of his marriage to Virginia Consett, he was appointed Solicitor General to Van Diemen's Land. He arrived at Hobart in 1825, the same year that his father was appointed the first puisne judge in New South Wales. His wife died in 1837 and in the following year he married Eleanor Bedford. By both marriages he had eighteen children. In 1839 he was appointed a puisne judge of the Supreme Court of New South Wales. He served as Chief Justice 1844-1873. He was knighted in 1846, made a Companion of the Bath in 1862, a K.C.M.G. in 1874, a G.C.M.G. in 1884 and a Privy Councillor in 1893.   **K.F.**

Item 189 (one of pair)

190 A fine and rare large snuff box, inscribed to "James Grant Esqre of Tullochgoram from the settlers of the Break 'o Day, Georges River 1835".

James Grant, the founder of Tullocgorum Fingal was born in Scotland, the son of the Reverend James Grant and named his property after his father's birthplace. In 1824 he chartered the vessel "Heroine" and with his wife and child sailed for Van Diemans Land with equipment for starting life in a new and savage land. James Grant introduced the Saxon and Spanish Merino sheep to Tasmania and played a big part in the development of the Fingal Valley, at one time the property totalled approximately 25,000 acres. He died in 1879.

> *MAKER: David Barclay, Tasmania. LENGTH: 7½ cm Width: 5 cm.*
> *CIRCA: 1835 Private Collection, Queensland.*
> *ILLUSTRATED*

191 An extremely fine and rare large presentation salver, heavily embossed and inscribed: "Presented to Anthony Fenn Kemp, Esq., by 150 of his fellow colonists, Hobart Town, Van Diemens Land, 1834". The back inscribed: "Manufactured in the colony by Mr D. Barclay, 1834" with the maker's mark in script.

> *MAKER: D. Barclay, Tasmania. LENGTH: 35 cm. WEIGHT: 44 ozs.*
> *CIRCA: 1834 Private Collection, Sydney.*
> *ILLUSTRATED*

Item 190

Item 191

QUEENSLAND SILVERSMITHS

FREDERICK JAMES MOLE

MOLE, Frederick James 549 Stanley Street, South Brisbane, established 1913 and continuing until 1957, registered his trade mark No. 19133 of 23rd November, 1915, of an M, Emu and Maltese cross, each in a square, for his manufactured goods in all sterling silver—vases, cups, bowls, serviette rings and communion vessels. (The Maltese Cross is part of the Queensland Flag). The business is now run by Kevin Eager, C. Best and Mrs Best.   **F.N.H.**

MARKS INDEX
INTRODUCTION

My initial plan was to photograph the marks on all the items exhibited in the form of a marks index for publication. The photographs, however, were not sufficiently detailed to provide a clear indication of the relevant marks and thanks to the skill of my wife, they are now here produced as line drawings and are faithful copies from the photographic originals. Where marks have been duplicated on certain items, the one which has been struck most clearly has been reproduced.

No consistent form of marking has ever applied in Australia. Australian silversmiths did not have access to an assay office, therefore, they had to create their own individual style of mark for their respective products. Certain silversmiths, such as Edwards, maintained the same marks throughout their working period. Others, such as Steiner and Dick, varied their marks considerably. It is from the dated inscriptions and the style of the item that an approximate sequence of marks in date order may be ascertained.

The index itself, with its additional notes, should be self-explanatory. However, I am aware that although these marks have been gleaned from over 300 items of Australian silver, the variations of certain makers' marks are, as yet, not complete. This, I feel, is a step in the right direction and I would be glad to hear from anyone who can provide a variation or a mark not contained in this index, preferably photographically.

J. B. Hawkins.

N.S.W. SILVERSMITHS' MARKS

MARKS REF. No.	CATALOGUE ITEM No.	MARKS	REMARKS	MARKS APPROX. USAGE DATE	MAKER	BUSINESS DATES
1.			In the original the kangaroo is badly struck and the mark is taken from the Macquarie trowel.	1821	S. Clayton	1817-34
2.	1		Marks for Glasgow, a kangaroo being substituted for the city mark.	1820	W. Harley	1820-21
3.	3		All marks other than the maker's mark bear a very close resemblance to marks 10, 11 and 12 of A. Dick.	1825	J. Robertson	1822-30
4.	5			1826	J. Robertson	
5.	4			1827	J. Robertson	
6.	6		From tray retailed by M. M. Cohen.	1835	H. Cohen	1829-Circa 1835
7.			From a mustard spoon not exhibited, the script H.C. is an attribution to Henry Cohen. The S.S. is common, Circa 1835, to marks 21 and 22.	1835	H. Cohen	1829-Circa 1835
8.	7		This signature is engraved in script to reverse of tray in conjunction with defaced marks that are possibly Anglo-Indian.	Circa 1844	J. J. Cohen	1839-53
9.			Mark from a lidded sugar bowl en suite with a spoon that was signed in full 'J. J. Cohen, N.S.W.'	Circa 1850	J. J. Cohen	1839-53
10.	9		Two basting spoons Allen canteen.	1827-29	A. Dick	1825-44
11.			Two spoons fiddle pattern owner's initials P.P.M.	1827-30	A. Dick	1825-44
12.	9 20		Balance of Allen canteen. The mug seems to be out of sequence as presentation inscription is for 1839.	1827-30	A. Dick	1825-44

MARKS REF. No.	CATALOGUE ITEM No.	REMARKS	MARKS APPROX. USAGE DATE	MAKER	BUSINESS DATES
13.		Carter canteen Mitchell Library, six teaspoons, balance of canteen by H. Twentyman, Calcutta.	1827-30	A. Dick	1825-44
14.	14 18	Note flaw in base of punch mark of castle. Both items of better quality.	Circa 1830-34	A. Dick	1825-44
15.	9	One spoon crested Allen but initialled R.E.A., again with flaw in castle.	Circa 1830-34	A. Dick	1825-44
16.	15 19	McDonald canteen part London maker W. Eaton 1837, balance Dick.	1837	A. Dick	1825-44
17.		Spoon initialled D.T.G.	Circa 1837	A. Dick	1825-44
18.	22	Struck on handle of trowel which is inscribed for 1839.	1839	A. Dick	1825-44
19.	12 17	Set of four labels and pap boat.	1835-40	A. Dick	1825-44
20.	23	From one of three teaspoons from this maker, the others private collection, Adelaide & Regan Collection, Tamworth.	Circa 1835	R. Broad	1833-42
21.	24	From the crest other items from this canteen may eventually be traced. Apart from the maker's mark, this and 22 are identical. The sterling silver S.S seems to have been a standard 1835-40 mark amongst Sydney silversmiths.	Circa 1835	F. Lynn	1830-40
22.	25		Circa 1840	A. Robertson	1833-47
23.	26	From the Plunkett entree dish attributed to Lamb.	Circa 1841	R. Lamb	1838-58

MARKS REF. No.	CATALOGUE ITEM No.	MARK	REMARKS	MARKS APPROX. USAGE DATE	MAKER	BUSINESS DATES
24.	31	C.L. QWIST · SYDNEY	He appears to have used only this one standard mark.	Circa 1870	C. Qwist	1864-77
25.	32	B & M.D	This mark occurs on all the separate parts of the mace.	Circa 1854	Brush & MacDonnell	1850-88
26.	57	WJM.D ⚓ ♣	Tentatively attributed to W. MacDonnell.	Circa 1850	W. MacDonnell	Circa 1850
27.	42 43	EVAN JONES SYDNEY	In the use of the emu egg, there is a stylistic similarity with Qwist's work, Circa 1870 (Item 29) and apart from the same shop address, there may be some connection.	Circa 1870	E. Jones	1870-92
28.	35	EVAN JONES	Standard mark used on majority of pieces.	1875-90	E. Jones	1870-92
29.	45	E J Hollingdale	Script signature on gold Crozier.	1877	E. J. Hollingdale	1859-82
30.	46	J.McLEAN MAKER SYDNEY	A standard mark found on a lot of Sydney church plate.	1860-94	J. McLean	1860-94
31.	47	W KERR	Standard mark with no variations.	1873-96	W. Kerr	1873-96
32.	54		No recorded mark, only engraved signature.	1885-92	J. H. Eaves	1885-92
33.		PROUD .925 🦘 F	This mark was in use in 1925-28 without the F. Late wares manufactured for them by W. J. Sanders include the F.	1925-28 1928-present	Prouds Ltd.	1912-

MARKS REF. No.	CATALOGUE ITEM No.	Mark	REMARKS	MARKS APPROX. USAGE DATE	MAKER	BUSINESS DATES
34.		W.J.S. 925 ● STG	W. J. Sanders, the last firm of manufacturing silversmiths in Sydney, manufacturers for David Jones Ltd., William Drummond & Co., Fairfax & Roberts and Hardy Bros., whose marks following were supplied by W. J. Sanders Pty. Ltd.	1911-present	W. J. Sanders	1911-present
35.		H B Rs STG	The H. Brs. mark is found in conjunction with English sterling marks, 1890-1920 and as illustrated for wares made in Australia.	1890-present	Hardy Bros.	1892-present
36.		D.J.Lᴰ ·925 STG	1920-present, mark on silver ware made for David Jones Ltd. by W. J. Sanders.	1920-present	David Jones Ltd.	1920-present
37.		F&R ● Ste	1920-present, mark on silver ware made for Fairfax & Roberts by W. J. Sanders.	1920-present	Fairfax & Roberts	1920-present

UNASCRIBED MARKS, N.S.W.

MARKS REF. No.	CATALOGUE ITEM No.	Mark	REMARKS	MARKS APPROX. USAGE DATE	MAKER	BUSINESS DATES
38.		WH i	From a set of six spoons, fiddle pattern, Circa 1820, possibly a variation of Harley's mark.			
39.		CN	Spoons in the Carter canteen Mitchell Library, possibly Anglo-Indian or Sydney, Circa 1840.			
40.		J· WA LK ER	Possibly J. Walker, partner in Walker & Jones, Circa 1860, or John F. Walker, Jeweller, 371 Bourke Street, Darlinghurst, both of whom may be one of the same. Mark taken from four spoons and struck in separate punches.			
41.			From a marrow scoop, dated stylistically to the 1840s, probably made in Sydney.			

SOUTH AUSTRALIAN SILVERSMITHS' MARKS

MARKS REF. No.	CATALOGUE ITEM No.	Marks	REMARKS	MARKS APPROX. USAGE DATE	MAKER	BUSINESS DATES
42.			From a spoon, Circa 1830s, fiddle pattern.			
43.	58		This minute mark requires considerable magnification to be readable and has many similarities both in size and consistency with those of Firnhaber.	1847	J. H. Pace	1842-50
44.	59		This mark is attributed to Schomberg, who was the only working silversmith in Adelaide at that date who has the same initials. There was, however, a John Smith, 93 Hindley St., Adelaide, Circa 1866. However, I do not think that the medal would be mounted as late as this.	Circa 1860	J. Schomberg	Circa 1850 Circa 1865
45. 46.	60 60		From the Royal Exchange Cup this and Mark 46 taken from the lid and base respectively. The marks must be for 1849 as the cup was presented in January, 1850.	1849	C. E. Firnhaber	1849-75
47.	61 62		These two items span a period of twelve years and it may be concluded that Firnhaber used this as a standard mark.	1851-63	C. E. Firnhaber	1849-75
48.	63		As for Mark No. 47 with the addition of the kangaroo. Taken from the Hanson Cup which is marked consistently throughout with this mark.	1862	C. E. Firnhaber	1849-75
49.	64a		Dated from inscription 1861, it bears what may be assumed to be the continental town mark for Steiner's home in Germany.	1861	H. Steiner	1860-84

MARKS REF. No.	CATALOGUE ITEM No.	Mark	REMARKS	MARKS APPROX. USAGE DATE	MAKER	BUSINESS DATES
50.		HST 14	Flatware, private collection, Adelaide.	1861	H. Steiner	1860-84
51.	73	HST 14	Although this item bears a presentation inscription for 1874 I suggest that it was made Circa 1865 (from the marks) for the Inter-Colonial Exhibition, Melbourne 1866, and may have been used as an advertising piece until sold in 1874.	Circa 1865	H. Steiner	1860-84
52.	65	H.S.t	Early mounted egg.	1862-65	H. Steiner	1860-84
53.	71	HST	A mounted emu egg of good quality.	Circa 1865	H. Steiner	1860-84
54.	64	HST	An interesting mark, it does not seem to follow the pattern of the others.	1861?	H. Steiner	1860-84
55.	68	HST	Inkwell.	Circa 1865	H. Steiner	1860-84
56.	72	HSt	Pair of early vases.	Circa 1865	H. Steiner	1860-64
57.	70	HST	Cast candle stick.	Circa 1875	H. Steiner	1860-84
58.	66	HST	Emu egg mounted as an ornament.	Circa 1865	H. Steiner	1860-84
59.	67	H.STEINER	Emu egg mounted as candle stick and snuffer.	Circa 1865-70	H. Steiner	1860-84

MARKS REF. No.	CATALOGUE ITEM No.	MARKS	REMARKS	MARKS APPROX. USAGE DATE	MAKER	BUSINESS DATES
60.	74		This trophy is earlier than the inscription.	Circa 1865-70	H. Steiner	1860-84
61.			An unusual variation of Steiner's mark.	Circa 1870	H. Steiner	1860-84
62.	78		An attribution to Steiner based on Mark No. 54.	Circa 1860-70	H. Steiner	1860-84
63.	76		Inscribed and dated trowel for 1875, it would appear that Steiner marked his name in full from the early 1870s.	1875	H. Steiner	1860-84
64.	77		Mounted emu egg claret jug.	Circa 1870-75	H. Steiner	1860-84
65.	79		Perfume bottle holder.	Circa 1875-80	H. Steiner	1860-84
66.	81		Chalice silver gilt.	Circa 1880	H. Steiner	1860-84
67.	92		Inscribed and dated trophy, for 1882. This mark seems to have been the standard from 1880 to 1884 for all Steiner's work.	Circa 1880-84	H. Steiner	1860-84
68.			From poor quality mounted emu egg not exhibited.	Circa 1865	J. M. Wendt	1860-1910
69.	106		A fine ostrich egg goblet.	Circa 1865-70	J. M. Wendt	1860-1910

MARKS REF. No.	CATALOGUE ITEM No.	REMARKS	MARKS APPROX. USAGE DATE	MAKER	BUSINESS DATES
70.	108	Tray inscribed and dated 1870.	1870	J. M. Wendt	1860-1910
71.	103	Presentation trophy inscribed and dated 1876.	Circa 1870-76	J. M. Wendt	1860-1910
72.	112	Three-piece tea service.	Circa 1880-90	J. M. Wendt	1860-1910
73.	113	Trowel inscribed and dated 1890.	Circa 1890-1900	J. M. Wendt	1860-1910
74.	115	Presentation inscription for 1901. This must be the last year of this mark with Queen Victoria's head.	Circa 1890-1900	J. M. Wendt	1860-1910
75.	118	Claret jug inscribed and dated 1898. The lion facing left.	Circa 1885-1900	A. Brunkhorst	1885-1919
76.	125	Presentation trophy inscribed and dated 1909.	Circa 1900-1910	A. Brunkhorst	1885-1919
77.		General mark for Brunkhorst with cut shoulders to lion punch. It should be noted that a lot of Steiner's work was sold by Brunkhorst in the initial stages of his business.		A. Brunkhorst	1885-1919
78.	127	Inscribed and dated claret jug for 1890.	Circa 1890	W. Stevenson	1878-Circa 1920
79.	128	A fine crested tray, this mark is probably the earlier mark but by the style of the tray would be Circa 1900. However, it may cover the period from 1880-1900. The addition of the lion and crown being missed from Mark No. 78.	Circa 1880-1900	W. Stevenson	1878-Circa 1920

MARKS REF. No.	CATALOGUE ITEM No.	MARK	REMARKS	MARKS APPROX. USAGE DATE	MAKER	BUSINESS DATES
80.		STEVENSON STG. SILVER	A variation on the above, from a card box not exhibited.	Circa 1900	W. Stevenson	1878-Circa 1920
81.		BASSE ADELAIDE SILVER	From a silver mounted snuff mull, the property of The Silver Lyon Ltd., Scotland, not exhibited. A general note: Late 19th century South Australian silver seems to have adopted almost standard marks of a lion rampant and crown.	Circa 1880-1900	F. Basse	1880-1900
82.	130	M.K.	A set of four wine labels attributed to M. Kendrick.	Circa 1910	M. Kendrick? Fidler & Kendrick?	Circa 1900-1920
83.		STG. SIL W K	Attributed to the Kendrick family, this mark found on two wine labels.	Circa 1910		

VICTORIAN SILVERSMITHS' MARKS

MARKS REF. No.	CATALOGUE ITEM No.	MARK	REMARKS	MARKS APPROX. USAGE DATE	MAKER	BUSINESS DATES
84.		BS & HS STG. SILVER	This mark taken from a waffling iron, inscribed 'The Lamb Inn Melbourne' which was opened June, 1837 and closed in 1843. The silversmith is unknown and at present untraceable but would be the earliest working silversmith in Victoria.	Circa 1840		
85.	131 132	Charles Bennett Melbourne Sterling Silver	This silversmith whose only mark is engraved in full on both items, obviously enjoyed the patronage of the Governor.	Circa 1835	C. Bennett	1840-50
86.	133	CB	A table snuff box inscribed and dated 1848.	1848	C. Brentani	1845-55

MARKS REF. No.	CATALOGUE ITEM No.	Marks	MARKS APPROX. USAGE DATE	REMARKS	MAKER	BUSINESS DATES
87.	136 140		1859-1865	Edwards' standard mark used on all his early work.	W. Edwards	1859-89
88.	139		1866-70	Claret jug presented as per inscription 1866, same marks as No. 87 with addition of Sterling Silver.	W. Edwards	1859-89
89.	160		1867	Royal Appointment mark in use only after 1867.	W. Edwards	1859-89
90.	142		1870-	In my opinion Edwards' business developed into a manufacturing business in the main after 1870.	W. Edwards	1859-89
91.	140		1859-65	Mark taken from a claret jug by Edwards retailed by Walsh & Sons, who seem to have sold a lot of Edwards' work.	Walsh & Sons	1859-65
92.	162		1866	From a set of finger bowls possibly again by Edwards but sold after the father's retirement and the change in business name in 1864 to Brs., not Sons. Inscribed and dated 1866.	Walsh Brs.	1865-81
93.	165		1864-81	Taken from a racing trophy inscribed and dated 1876.	Walsh Brs.	1865-81
94.	169		Circa 1880	Model cradle marked in full.	G. H. Armfield	1878-1900
95.	170		1880	Fischer's only mark and is common to all his work, from gold cup inscribed and dated 1880.	E. F. Fischer	1858-1916
96.	176		Circa 1880-90	Jug marked 'H. Young & Comp.' The jug inscribed and dated 1883.	H. Young	

MARKS REF. No.	CATALOGUE ITEM No.	MARK	REMARKS	MARKS APPROX. USAGE DATE	MAKER	BUSINESS DATES
97.	180	DRUMMOND MELBOURNE	Model emu paper weight, probably made by Kilpatrick and retailed by Drummonds.	Circa 1900	Drummond	Circa 1880-Circa 1910
98.		W.D. & Cº. 925 STG	20th Cent. mark used by manufacturers such as W. J. Sanders for Drummonds' work.	1910-present	Drummonds	1910-present
99.			McBean name stamped in full 'J. McBean & Son'.		J. McBean & Son	1860s-90s
100.	179	K&Co STERLING SILVER	Standard mark: on kangaroo paper weights.	Circa 1890	Kilpatrick & Co.	1861-1902
101.	166	HAMMERTON GEELONG	Poorly made trophy.	Circa 1890	J. Hammerton & Son	1880-1927
102.	167	DENIS BROS STG.SILVER	Pair of mounted emu egg jugs.	Circa 1890	Denis Bros.	1865-Circa 1900
103.	168	STG. SIL. D.B.S. MELB.	A very fine chalice.	Circa 1880	Denis Bros.	1865-Circa 1900
104.		STG SILVER BRADSHAW	Firm of 20th Cent. silversmiths.	Circa 1900-1914	Bradshaw	
105.		BRADSHAW STG SIL	Mark used Circa 1920.			
106.		STG SIL	See notes in catalogue under 'Stokes' for marks. This drawing of the mark registered 1920 is the only one seen by me, to date.			

UNASCRIBED MARKS, POSSIBLY VICTORIAN

MARKS REF. No.	CATALOGUE ITEM No.	MARKS	REMARKS	MARKS APPROX. USAGE DATE	MAKER	BUSINESS DATES
107.			Silver mounted emu egg, Circa 1875.			

TASMANIAN SILVERSMITHS' MARKS

MARKS REF. No.	CATALOGUE ITEM No.	MARKS	REMARKS	MARKS APPROX. USAGE DATE	MAKER	BUSINESS DATES
108.	191		Marked and dated salver for 1834 with date letter 'O' the 'D.B.' in script.	1834	D. Barclay	1831-Circa 1850
109.	189		Marked and dated pair of salvers for 1839 (April) if actually constructed in 1838 we would have a date letter sequence of 1834 O 1835 P this, however, 1836 Q is purely 1837 R supposition. 1838 S	1839	D. Barclay	1831-Circa 1850

QUEENSLAND SILVERSMITHS' MARKS

MARKS REF. No.	CATALOGUE ITEM No.	MARKS	REMARKS	MARKS APPROX. USAGE DATE	MAKER	BUSINESS DATES
110.		 STERLING SILVER	Most of their items were small practical objects and they used this one standard mark.	1913-present	F. J. Mole	1913-present

WESTERN AUSTRALIAN SILVERSMITHS

The Linton family were Western Australia's leading silversmiths. James Walter Robert Linton, 1869-1948, came to Western Australia in 1893, founded the first School of Art in the Perth Technical College, exhibited with the Royal Institute of Water Colour 1908-1910. Exhibited silver in Sydney 1935, see Art in Australia 1935. His silver mark was of a gum nut with the initals 'J.W.L.'.

His son, James Alexander Barrow Linton, born 1904, also a silversmith. His mark is the gum nut with the initials 'J.A.L.'.

His son, John Linton, presently studying design and style at the Royal College of Art, London.